No Ordinary Task

Hidden Stories from West Virginia's History

By Bryan Ward and Catherine Breese

Alta Blue Skies Publishing

ISBN: 0692465383
ISBN-13: 978-0692465387

DEDICATION

To our dog, Henry Huffington.

Henry was beloved by many. Caring for him was like the title of this book, No Ordinary Task. *He was one of a kind that required hundreds of years of indiscriminate breeding to produce the finest West Virginia White Dog we have ever encountered.*

CONTENTS

Acknowledgements

Like the title of this book this collection of essays has been *No Ordinary Task*. The help and guidance of many made it possible.

The impetus of this project began with a request of Jennifer Jett Prezkop who asked Bryan to write an article for *West Virginia Executive*. Since that time we have written articles for the magazine several of which appear in this collection. Jennifer was great to work with and suggested several topics that brought unknown topics to light.

Several of the articles appear in *Wonderful West Virginia* Magazine. Shelia McEntee, thank you very much.

The research for these articles was conducted at the West Virginia State Archives that is a treasure that every Mountaineer should celebrate and visit often. The staff led by Joe Geiger are wonderful and we feel fortunate to have worked with them. Any serious researcher or historian of West Virginia history should take advantage of their knowledge and expertise.

We also wish to thank Phillip Bird who gave the manuscript a critical read-through. He was most diligent and thorough even on very short time schedule.

We would also like our families that have encouraged us throughout the process and were always there to support us in everything we do. Especially our children, Carty, Zack, Abbey and Jack who help keep us grounded and the world in its proper perspective.

Bryan Ward, Jr. and Catherine Breese

Introduction

It does not take long for a person from West Virginia to share a bit of the state's history with anyone who will listen. Even those who move to the state will quickly and unavoidably begin to educate outsiders and flat-landers. If you are from West Virginia you are probably thinking about several bits of information that you are willing to share right now.

This love for the state's history is passed down through family members. It starts on front porches or in living rooms and eventually leads to road trips and tramping through the woods to see important sites. We can't help it. We stop and read the state's highway historical markers and commit them to memory. Great pride is taken in not only what one knows about the state, but also in actually visiting the historical location. In 8th grade the students of West Virginia embark on West Virginia history. For many, this is the most important class their children will take. For many children of West Virginia their greatest regret is that they did not win a Golden Horseshoe. In fact, Bryan receives a regular reminder/taunt, usually on June 20, that he, in fact, did not win that coveted prize. Other states just aren't like that.

With this book, the hope is that several more stories can be added to the lexicon of West Virginia history. These articles appeared in *Wonderful West Virginia*, *West Virginia Executive*, and in an online exhibit for West Virginia Archives and History website. The topics include West Virginia Statehood, the Golden Horseshoe, the 1960 West Virginia Presidential Primary, artificial limbs, petrochemicals, the salt industry, penicillin, glass, and the New Deal.

These articles tell a story that many West Virginians know and other people need to hear. They tell stories of innovators, strivers, and the extraordinary people who refuse to give up.

Montani Semper Liberi,
Bryan Ward and Catherine Breese
June 20, 2015

Bryan Ward, Jr. and Catherine Breese

1

NO ORDINARY TASK

THE STOUT HEARTS THAT CREATED WEST VIRGINIA, PART 1[1]

West Virginia's path to statehood was, as the state's first governor, Arthur I. Boreman, described it, "no ordinary task." In spite of the myriad challenges, a group of men risked their reputations, their riches, and their very lives to navigate that path. In honor of their efforts—and in celebration of the West Virginia's 150th anniversary—this article and a subsequent one will examine the contributions of six individuals who played principal roles in the creation of the great state of West Virginia. In this first installment, we will examine three statesmen.

In the 1860s, many western Virginians believed that they had been getting a raw deal. Even as the population in the western part of the state expanded, representation in Richmond favored eastern planters. Calls for internal improvements and free public education—two subjects of great interest in the west—fell on deaf ears in the General Assembly. While reforms in the 1850s had addressed some issues of concern, three decades of frustration still simmered under the surface. From this frustration a new

---

[1] *A version of this article appeared in the January 2013 issue of* Wonderful West Virginia *Magazine.*

generation of political leaders emerged in the west. When faced with a choice of Confederacy or Union, they went Union. Waitman T. Willey, John S. Carlile, and Arthur I. Boreman were three of the leaders who chose the Union and who, in turn, made West Virginia statehood possible.

In 1860, as the desire for secession gripped the deep South after the election of Abraham Lincoln, Virginia's first stance was one of moderation. Delegates were selected and called to Richmond to discuss what Virginia's position on secession should be. Two of the delegates who attended that meeting would be essential to the creation of West Virginia. Ironically, one was described by the pro-Union and Republican Wheeling Intelligencer as not having "the backbone for times like these." The other ultimately destroyed his political career and forever has been seen as a traitor to the statehood cause.

When Harrison County delegate John S. Carlile arrived in Richmond for the Secession Convention, he had one goal in mind: that Virginia remain firmly in the Union. While Southern firebrands like former Governor Henry Wise shouted for the cause of secession, Carlile responded by calling the breakaway "self-murder" and "an insult to all living humanity and a crime against God." Carlile's style won him few friends among secessionists in Richmond. He was accosted on the street, and one evening he heard shouts from the lawn of his boarding house. A rowdy crowd had gathered there and thrown a noose over the branch of a tree to demonstrate their displeasure. Stubborn and undeterred, Carlile stuck to his convictions.

Joining Carlile in Richmond was Monongalia County delegate Waitman T. Willey. Willey was firmly pro-Union, but his style differed from the verbose Carlile. Willey warned the delegates at Richmond that if Virginia chose secession, the result would be a division of the state.

Fort Sumter a Turning Point

On April 12, 1861, with the Confederate bombardment of

Fort Sumter and the subsequent evacuation of federal troops there, the mood of the convention was transformed. In response to the Confederate action, President Lincoln made a call for 75,000 troops to put down the rebellion. When word reached Richmond that Virginia would have a quota of troops to supply for the effort, any hope for Virginia to remain in the Union was lost. On April 17, the delegates passed an Ordinance of Secession by a vote of 88 to 55. However, to take effect, the ordinance had to be ratified by a statewide vote, scheduled for May 23. Following the ordinance vote, Carlile, Willey, and others who voted against secession quickly left Richmond and returned home; their only hope lay in defeating secession at the ballot box.

Once he returned to Clarksburg, Carlile quickly organized a very large pro-Union rally. On April 22, approximately 1,200 people gathered at the Harrison County Courthouse to voice their opposition to secession. In their resolutions they called for the election of delegates, who would meet in Wheeling on May 13 to determine the actions of the people of northwestern Virginia. Carlile was the first person named to Harrison County's delegation. After the meeting, he attended other pro-Union rallies to protest secession and to share with the crowds his plan of a new state.

Waitman T. Willey and other delegates from 27 Virginia counties were present with Carlile for the convention in Wheeling on May 13. Although Carlile and Willey had been united by their cause in Richmond, a rift between them quickly developed. Willey, Gen. John Jay Jackson of Wood County, and most of the delegates believed that the best course of action was to wait for the results of the statewide vote on secession, which was 10 days away. Carlile and others believed that the time for action was at hand. Carlile offered a resolution that called for the creation of the state of New Virginia. After vigorous debate and much political wrangling, Carlile accepted defeat. In an uncharacteristically conciliatory act, he joined the others to approve a resolution that condemned secession and called for another meeting in Wheeling on June 11, if the Ordinance of Secession was approved by voters.

When the Ordinance of Secession prevailed, pro-Union delegates returned to Wheeling with a more deliberate purpose. Arthur I. Boreman of Parkersburg was selected to be the president of the new convention. When he spoke to the delegates, he said that the task they were faced with would require "stout hearts" and "men of courage" to carry out. At this meeting Carlile did not call for a new state but instead submitted a declaration that called for the reorganization of the Government of Virginia with a new slate of government officials. This action created two Virginias: one Confederate, with its capital in Richmond, and one Union, with its capital in Wheeling. After the passage of the proposal, Francis Pierpont of Marion County was elected governor.

In the weeks that followed, the Restored Government of Virginia in Wheeling met and John Carlile and Waitman T. Willey were named its U.S. Senators. While Carlile was an obvious choice, Willey's election drew the ire of Archibald Campbell of the Wheeling Intelligencer, who lambasted the choice in his paper. Campbell questioned Willey's leadership and his fortitude. As far as Campbell was concerned, Willey's willingness to compromise was a danger to the Union and statehood.

A New and Independent State

On August 6, 1861, delegates returned to Wheeling after a recess. When convention president Arthur I. Boreman called the convention to order, the plan was to create a new and independent State. After a week of debate on the issue, the convention passed an ordinance for the creation of the new state of "Kanawha," which would consist of 39 counties, plus Berkeley, Greenbrier, Hampshire, Hardy, Jefferson, Morgan, and Pocahontas, if a majority of voters in those counties approved. On October 24, voters approved the division.

In November, delegates returned to Wheeling—this time to write a constitution. Though voters had approved the name "Kanawha," a lengthy and comical debate concluded with the selection of the name West Virginia.

Now the new state had been established and named, but its boundaries were still a major problem, and the issue of slavery truly divided the convention. After considerable discussion, the final result was a compromise that stated that "no slave shall be brought, or free person of color be permitted to come into this State for permanent residence." Basically, delegates had agreed to ban African American settlement. The final constitution was approved unanimously by the delegates and later approved, by a large measure, by the voters.

On May 29, 1862, Waitman T. Willey presented West Virginia's formal petition for statehood to the U.S. Senate. The petition was forwarded to the Senate's Committee on Territories, where John S. Carlile was tasked with writing the statehood bill. When the bill emerged from committee, Willey and other statehood proponents were stunned. Carlile had added 15 counties, provided for gradual emancipation of slaves, and called for a new constitutional convention—all of which threatened passage of the bill entirely.

Yet Willey responded with an amendment that rescued the bill. The West Virginia Bill with the Willey Amendment, as it was known, called for the creation of a West Virginia that would gradually emancipate slaves. With the amendment the bill passed by a vote of 23 to 17. Carlile aggressively argued against the bill and the Willey Amendment and, in the end, actually voted against statehood. However, after a fierce debate in the House of Representatives, the bill passed by a vote of 96 to 55.

When Lincoln finally received the West Virginia Bill, he agonized over it. In an effort to get a broader opinion, he had his cabinet review the matter to provide him with other perspectives. His cabinet split evenly on the question's constitutionality and expediency of the West Virginia bill. But after some lobbying from Willey and Congressmen William G. Brown and Jacob Blair, Lincoln ultimately supported the creation of West Virginia.

After receiving presidential approval, the constitutional convention returned to Wheeling and added the Willey

Amendment's gradual emancipation clause to the state's constitution. John Carlile and other former statehood supporters continued to fight the West Virginia Bill and especially the Willey Amendment. After voter approval, Lincoln designated June 20, 1863, as the date West Virginia would join the Union.

Following statehood, Arthur I. Boreman became West Virginia's first governor and guided the state during its most precarious period. After being elected governor for three terms, he served West Virginia in the U.S. Senate. Waitman T. Willey no longer served the Restored Government of Virginia but instead became one of West Virginia's U.S. Senators. John Carlile's political career was ruined in West Virginia. Carlile supported Republican Ulysses S. Grant for president and was awarded with a nomination to be a minister to Sweden. However, the nomination was blocked by Republicans in the Senate after numerous West Virginians objected to it. On October 24, 1878, Carlile died and was later buried in the Odd Fellows Cemetery in Clarksburg. Even after his death bitterness remained. It took two days for the Wheeling Intelligencer, which once championed Carlile, to write his obituary and announce his death.

2

NO ORDINARY TASK

THE STOUT HEARTS THAT CREATED WEST VIRGINIA,
Part 2[2]

A chieving statehood for West Virginia was, in the words of the state's first governor, Arthur I. Boreman, "no ordinary task." In spite of the myriad challenges, a group of men risked their reputations, their riches, and their very lives to achieve that goal. In honor of their efforts, and in celebration of the West Virginia's 150th anniversary, this article, the second installment of a two part series, will examine three radicals whose actions and words changed the course of our state's history.

When Francis Pierpont of Marion County reached college age in 1835, there wasn't an institution of higher education in Virginia west of the Allegheny Mountains. In order to receive a higher degree, Pierpont, like others in western Virginia, looked to Allegheny College in Meadville, Pennsylvania. The school, affiliated

---

[2] *A version of this article appeared in the February 2013 issue of* Wonderful West Virginia *Magazine.*

with the Methodist Episcopal Church, attracted students from across the Ohio Valley. One of those students, Gordon Battelle, dined with Pierpont regularly.

Pierpont received his degree from Allegheny in 1839 and Battelle earned his the following year. After college, both men became teachers. In the years that followed, Pierpont became a lawyer in Fairmont. Battelle became a Methodist pastor with a strong commitment to education.

While in college, Francis Pierpont developed outstanding oratory and debating skills. Those skills served him well in the courtroom and in the court of public opinion. During the 1840s, he became involved with the Whig Party, which had formed in opposition to the policies of Andrew Jackson and the Democratic Party. In support of his party, Pierpont penned biting attacks that were published in a number of Whig newspapers in western Virginia. Stung by his rhetoric, the Democratic press labeled Pierpont a radical "black Republican," "abolitionist," and, in one comical editorial, "the big-bellied slander of Fairmont."

One paper that carried Pierpont's attacks was a new Republican daily paper in Wheeling, the *Daily Intelligencer*. In 1855, John McDermont and upstart Archibald Campbell took over the *Intelligencer* from the paper's founder. Campbell was a generation younger that Pierpont and Battelle and had gravitated to the newly formed Republican Party. When the Whig Party splintered over slavery, Pierpont was left looking for a new party, but he was unwilling to take the leap to the Republicans. Instead, he supported the Constitutional Union Party in hopes of keeping the Union together. Campbell and the Intelligencer bravely endorsed Abraham Lincoln for President; indeed, it was the only paper in Virginia to do so. Over the next few years, the *Intelligencer* would become the most militant paper in Virginia and the mouthpiece for the statehood movement.

Virginia Secedes from the Union

Abraham Lincoln was soundly defeated in Virginia, but nationally he won the presidency. States in the Deep South responded by seceding from the Union. Initially Virginia's stance was more moderate than those states further south. Through some political maneuvering, however, firebrands who supported secession were able to get a convention called in Richmond. By the time the convention met, seven states had already left the Union. For several months the convention supported the Union, but after two important events—South Carolina cannons firing on Fort Sumter and Lincoln calling for troops to put down the rebellion—the convention passed an Ordinance of Secession, which required a statewide referendum on May 23. When news of the ordinance reached western Virginia, Francis Pierpont joined with the most vocal anti-secessionist, John S. Carlile, to condemn the actions of the Richmond Convention. After mass meetings were held, a convention was called for in Wheeling to discuss the situation and to plan for further actions.

On the eve of the convention, Francis Pierpont delivered a rousing speech in favor of the Union that caused the *Intelligencer* to proclaim, "A truer man to the cause of the Union does not live." Though Carlile called for the formation of a new state on the second day of the convention, a majority thought the proposition was premature. Behind the scenes Pierpont was able to persuade the volatile Carlile that the secession referendum needed to take place. If Virginia went for secession, the delegates would return to Wheeling to chart a new course.

As part of the compromise, Pierpont, Carlile, and others were named to a central committee that remained in Wheeling. Pierpont had planned to return to Fairmont for the secession vote, but a visitor from Fairmont told him that Confederate troops had moved into the area. To minimize his risk, Pierpont devised a plan whereby a friend would send a telegram instructing Pierpont to "buy the sugar" if it was safe to go to Fairmont or "don't buy," if it was too dangerous. Pierpont returned to Fairmont on May 18 to find that his children had whooping cough. While he was getting wood in the middle of the night to feed the home fires, Pierpont's neighbor informed him that his name was mentioned among those of people to be arrested. Covertly, he left Fairmont. On May 23, Virginia voters approved the Ordinance of Secession. It was later revealed that many of the ballots from the west were never counted.

On June 11, 1861, the delegates returned to Wheeling and formed the pro-Union Restored Government of Virginia. On June 20, the convention unanimously elected Francis Pierpont as governor. Pierpont bravely took the reins of a state that was in open rebellion and without a military to defend itself or any treasury to fund its operations. In the months that followed, he coerced loans from several local Wheeling banks—loans that he and Parkersburg attorney and president of the Northwestern Virginia Railroad, Peter Van Winkle, personally guaranteed. He also obtained federal funds that the Virginia Legislature had previously refused to accept. Additionally, he sent soldiers to capture money held in a Weston bank for use in the construction of the Trans-Allegheny Lunatic Asylum. Through Pierpont's efforts, the Restored Government remained financially viable, and thus the statehood movement could go forward.

After voters approved the creation of a new state, a convention was called to write a constitution. After much discussion, the name "Kanawha," which had been approved by the voters during the referendum, was abandoned and West Virginia was chosen. Rev. Gordon Battelle charted a progressive course for the education of citizens in West Virginia by securing a provision in the constitution for free public schools. He also introduced a resolution that would prevent slaves from being brought into the new state and would gradually emancipate West Virginia slaves. This controversial measure was immediately tabled. Ultimately the constitutional compromise read: "No slave shall be brought, or free person of color be permitted to come into this State for permanent residence."

Senate Requires Emancipation

Battelle and Campbell were upset by the outcome. Campbell expressed his displeasure in the *Intelligencer* and warned that the measure could doom the state in Congress. Battelle voiced his disapproval in a pamphlet called "An Address to the Constitutional Convention and the People of West Virginia." Voters later approved the constitution, and Pierpont and the Restored Government gave their blessing. The fate of statehood was then left in the hands of the United States Congress.

As Campbell had warned, the United States Senate required that gradual emancipation be added to the state's constitution before West Virginia could become a state. Battelle must have been gratified to learn that his proposal for gradual emancipation was added to the bill. Unfortunately, Battelle would not live to see West Virginia achieve statehood. Less than a month after the bill passed the Senate, he was stricken with typhoid fever and died at the age of 48.

On December 10, 1862, the House of Representatives approved statehood with gradual emancipation and sent the bill to President Lincoln. Lincoln, concerned about the constitutionality of the bill, asked his cabinet to discuss the measure. The members split evenly on the matter and it appeared to all concerned that the bill may be vetoed.

At the encouragement of Archibald Campbell, Pierpont agreed to send one final telegram. With Campbell sitting at the governor's desk and Pierpont pacing around the room, they composed these words: "President Lincoln: I am in great hope you will sign the bill to make West Virginia a new State. The loyal troops from Virginia have their hearts set on it; the loyal people in the bounds of the new state have their hearts set on it; and if the bill fails, God only knows the result. I fear general demoralization and I must not be held responsible."

The telegram worked. Pierpont later reported that Lincoln told him that it was the telegram that helped him make the final decision. In his own justification for statehood, Lincoln wrote, "We can scarcely dispense with the aid of West Virginia in this struggle; much less can we afford to have her against us, in Congress and in the field. Her brave and good men regard her admission into the Union as a matter of life and death. They have been true to the Union under very severe trials. We have so acted as to justify their hopes, and we cannot fully retain their confidence, and cooperation, if we seem to break faith with them. In fact, they could not do so much for us, if they would."

West Virginia was welcomed to the Union on June 20, 1863. The importance of Francis Pierpont, Rev. Gordon Battelle, and Archibald Campbell in the state's formation cannot be overstated. Campbell gave the statehood movement its voice and kept it going forward in challenging and dangerous times. Without Pierpont's leadership, the fledgling state might not have made it through the early days of the war. And Battelle's moral guidance on the issues of education and slavery guided West Virginia's citizenry toward a more enlightened future. Along with Waitman T. Willey, Arthur I. Boreman, and John S. Carlile, these stalwart men made the nearly impossible idea of West Virginia possible.

3

The Struggle for Statehood[3]

When Abraham Lincoln was elected President on November 6, 1860, southern states erupted with calls for secession. By the time Virginia responded to the pending crisis, seven states had already left the Union. When delegates arrived in Richmond a majority of the delegates did not support secession. Some, like former Governor Henry A. Wise, vehemently called for disunion. Others, like John S. Carlile, boisterously stumped for Virginia to remain in the Union.

Carlile, a Clarksburg lawyer and former state senator, met every call for secession with a fierce rebuttal. During debates Carlile referred to the crisis as a Southern conspiracy that would result in "self-murder." He called secession "an insult to all living humanity, and a crime against God." His views, however, weren't universally well received in Richmond. Carlile was accosted on the

---

[3] *A version of this article appeared in the Fall 2012 issue of* West Virginia Executive *Magazine.*

street, and at one point, a rowdy crowd with a noose gathered outside his boarding house to share their displeasure with him.

Another staunch Unionist at the convention was Morgantown lawyer Waitman T. Willey who also challenged secession. While Carlile evoked the Almighty in his dramatic attacks, Willey calmly and prophetically warned the delegates gathered in Richmond that secession would eventually lead to a division of the state. On April 4, Carlile and Willey were united with the majority when they voted down a motion for secession, but, within weeks, they would find themselves precariously in the minority.

When Confederate forces fired on Fort Sumter on April 12, 1861, and Lincoln called for 75,000 troops to put down the rebellion, the mood of the convention shifted. Delegates quickly passed an Ordinance of Secession by a vote of 88 to 55. With the passage of the measure, Virginia's secession was then placed in the hands of the voters who would vote on the measure on May 23. Fearing for their lives, Carlile, Willey and the others who had voted against secession quickly left town and returned home to mobilize against secession.

Citizens in western Virginia gathered to voice their opposition to secession. One of the largest pro-Union gatherings occurred in Clarksburg on Monday, April 22. Nearly 1,200 people gathered at the courthouse. At the meeting led by Carlile and others, the convention issued a proclamation that challenged the actions of the Richmond Secession Convention and called for a convention of pro-Union delegates to meet in Wheeling on May 13.

On May 13, 1861, the First Wheeling Convention opened at Washington Hall. Two camps quickly developed. General John Jay Jackson, Willey and a majority of the delegates were willing to wait for the vote on the Secession Ordinance on May 23. Carlile and others, however, were ready for action and called for the formation of the state of New Virginia which would remain loyal to the Union. In spite of his efforts, Carlile's motion failed. In an uncharacteristic move, Carlile temporarily abandoned his statehood position and joined with the others to support the resolution that condemned secession and called for delegates to return to Wheeling if the secession ordinance passed.

When voters did, in fact, ratify secession, the delegates returned to Wheeling and selected Arthur I. Boreman of Parkersburg as president of the convention. On June 13, Carlile presented "A Declaration of the People of Virginia" that called for a reorganization of the state government with a new slate of state officials. Carlile abandoned his earlier call for statehood, and instead, moved to create a pro-Union government at Wheeling with the hope of forming a new state later. The ordinance was passed and on June 20, 1861, and the Restored Government of Virginia took shape with Francis Pierpont selected as governor. With the move Virginia now had two governments—one Confederate in Richmond and one that was loyal to the Union in Wheeling. On July 9, Waitman T. Willey and John S. Carlile were selected as the state's two U.S. Senators.

For many, like Archibald Campbell, editor of the Wheeling Daily Intelligencer, John Carlile was the best suited for the task at hand, but for Waitman Willey they had a harsher appraisal. Campbell said that he would have rather had any one of the other two candidates that ran against Willey. He felt that Willey was "a man of good enough abilities, experience and good character," but "not, never was, nor never will be a leader." He further lamented that Willey did not have "the backbone for times like these." After some initial wrangling and a heated debate in the U.S. Senate, Carlile and Willey were seated, nonetheless.

In August the Reorganized Government of Virginia met and approved a referendum for the creation of a new state. On October 24, voters approved the measure. In November a meeting was convened to write a constitution for the new state. The constitution was completed in February, but the question of slavery loomed large. The final result was a compromise provision that prohibited free blacks or slaves from permanent settlement in the state, a provision that would come back to haunt statehood leaders. Voters approved the new constitution on April 3, 1862. On May 13, the Reorganized Government of Virginia approved the creation of the new state. With the local hurdles completed, the measure now moved on for approval by Congress and President Lincoln.

On May 29, 1862, Willey presented the formal petition to the Senate for the admission of West Virginia to the Union. The petition was forwarded to the Committee on Territories where Carlile was tasked with writing the bill.

When Senator Benjmain Wade of Ohio reported the West Virginia Bill to the Senate on June 23, Willey and the statehood supporters in Wheeling were stunned. The bill drafted by Carlile was vastly different from what they had expected. Carlile had added 15 counties, provided for gradual emancipation and called for a new state constitutional convention. Willey moved quickly and offered an amendment to the bill to rectify the damage. After some compromise the Willey Amendment, as it became known, called for West Virginia statehood with the gradual emancipation of slaves, if the state constitutional convention approved of the measure.

Carlile bristled at any attempt of the federal government to impose conditions on the state. He openly opposed and argued against the Willey Amendment and actually voted against the statehood bill. In spite of Carlile's vote against the measure, the bill passed the Senate by a vote of 23 to 17 on July 14. Ironically, it had been over a year since the Wheeling *Daily Intelligencer* questioned Willey's resolve in manner of statehood, but it was he alone that rescued the West Virginia bill in the Senate. With passage in the Senate, the bill moved on to the House of Representatives. After another contentious debate the measure passed the House on December 10 by a vote of 96 to 55.

When the West Virginia bill first made its way to the White House, President Lincoln lamented to Illinois Senator Orville Browning that he wished he had more time to consider the bill. Under the Constitution Lincoln had 10 days to approve, veto, or let the bill become law without his signature. Browning, sensing the President's concerns, offered to delay delivery of the bill for a week, which he did after providing the president with an "unofficial" copy.

A week later, on December 22, 1862, President Lincoln was officially presented with the West Virginia statehood bill. Lincoln sent a copy of the bill to his cabinet members and asked them whether the act was constitutional and expedient. The cabinet split evenly with three in support of the bill and three against it. Unfortunately for Lincoln, the final decision would rest with him alone.

When word of Lincoln's plan to ask for opinions from his cabinet reached Willey and Congressmen William G. Brown and Jacob B. Blair, they hurriedly met with three members of Lincoln's cabinet. On December 31, the three met with Lincoln himself. During the meeting Lincoln read the opinions of his cabinet without revealing the authors' names, but Willey, Brown and Blair were well aware where each member stood. Finally, Lincoln shared his view and then bid them farewell until to the next day when his decision would be made.

Early the following morning, Congressman Jacob Blair made his way to the White House to learn of Lincoln's decision. When he arrived, the White House was closed because it was New Year's Day. Blair, unable to wait, found an open window and climbed inside. When he found Lincoln, who had just woken up, Lincoln went to his desk and retrieved the bill. He showed Blair the signed West Virginia Bill. An elated Blair thanked the president and quickly made his way to find Willey. After sharing the news, the two men rushed off to telegraph the results to Wheeling.

The West Virginia Constitutional Convention reconvened, approved the Willey Amendment, and set a state referendum vote for March 26. Carlile and others continued fight and urged voters to vote against the changes, but the measure passed. On June 20, 1863, to much fanfare West Virginia entered the Union as the 35th state.

Following statehood, the loyal Restored Government of Virginia and Governor Francis Pierpont moved to Alexandria where he was re-elected, and later became the Governor of Virginia during Reconstruction. Waitman Willey became a Senator for West Virginia where he served until 1871. To this day, historians continue to debate Carlile's tragic transformation from the state's most ardent proponent, to its great traitor.

4

West Virginia Independence Hall
A Witness to West Virginia Statehood[4]

West Virginia's path to statehood is very unlike any other state in the Union. The state was forged during the bloody American Civil War. As the state's first governor, Arthur I. Boreman adeptly described it, West Virginia was a "child of the rebellion". When leaders in Virginia decided to cast her lot with the Confederacy, a band of brave men met in Wheeling to reorganize a pro-Union government. With recognition as the "official" Virginia government in Washington and little else, Reorganized Governor of Virginia Francis Pierpont and others readied the state for war. The new political leaders of *western* Virginia navigated through a series of conventions, referendums, congressional debates and political compromises to create West Virginia. While the people that helped create the state now live only in annals of history and on memorials that bear their names, the Wheeling Custom House, today known as West Virginia Independence Hall, stands as a witness to the state's creation and

---

[4]*A version of this article appeared in the Winter 2013 issue of* West Virginia Executive *Magazine.*

early history.

It was cause for great fanfare when the Wheeling Custom House opened in 1859 as the headquarters for federal offices, the courtroom for the Western District of Virginia, and a U.S. Post Office. The building culminated Wheeling's decades of development and its prominence as a transportation hub. The city was uniquely positioned at the intersection of the National Road, the Ohio River, and the Baltimore and Ohio Railroad. The railroad was completed on Christmas Eve 1852, thus linking the eastern seaboard to Wheeling and points west.

The Wheeling Custom House was designed by Treasury Architect Ammi B. Young, who described his building as "Italianate with Greek details". Today, the style is known as Renaissance Revival. While the exterior of the building is reflective of the style prominent in the antebellum era, the interior structure is unique. In the 1850s, fires were a real and serious concern. In the 1850s, with large numbers of wood frame buildings and few tools and equipment to fight flames, even small fires could engulf entire cities. Even brick and stone building were threatened because of the use of wood in their support structures. For the Wheeling Custom House Young took advantage of a new material for the structure—wrought iron I-beams. The beams, first rolled at the Trenton Iron Works in 1854, became the skeleton of the new building and with the cast iron doors and shutters would be a defense against the threat of fire. While the threat of fire was Young's main concern in 1859, in the years that followed the primary concern was an attack by hostile military forces.

While many of the Southern states were quick to leave the Union following the election of Abraham Lincoln in 1860, leaders in Virginia were initially reluctant to join the Confederacy. In months following the election, leaders from around Virginia gathered in Richmond to discuss the pending crisis. At first, delegates to the convention took a moderate stance and leaned toward remaining in the Union. That stance changed, however, when President Lincoln called for troops following the bombing of

Ft. Sumter on April 12, 1861. Within days, the Richmond convention passed an ordinance rescinding Virginia's ratification of the Constitution and put final approval of secession before the voters on May 23. Delegates from western Virginia who voted against secession quickly fled Richmond under threat of violence. Once they returned to the west, they began to mobilize to thwart secession and push for Virginia to remain in the Union.

While much of Virginia prepared for war ahead of the secession vote, political leaders in the west met at Washington Hall in Wheeling on May 13, 1861. At the convention the rancorous western Congressman, John S. Carlile, moved for the creation of a new state. Carlile found vocal support for his measure, but his supporters remained in the minority as others at the meeting called for patience and held out hope for the secession measure to fail the statewide referendum. When voters approved secession, delegates returned to Wheeling on July 1, 1861, to charter a different course.

On July 13, 1861, a second Wheeling convention met in the courtroom of the Wheeling Custom House for the first time. During the day's proceedings, John Carlisle presented "A Declaration of the People of Virginia," which stated that the actions of the secession convention in Richmond were illegal. It declared that offices held by Confederate sympathizers were vacant. The declaration also called for the convention to elect a new governor and other state officials. On June 20, 1861, the convention elected Fairmont-native Francis Pierpont as governor. Pierpont and the other newly elected officials made their offices in the Wheeling Custom House. The building had become the *de facto* pro-Union capitol of the Reorganized Government of Virginia.

In the years that followed the Wheeling Custom House witnessed the call for a new state, the formation the new state's constitution, and the proceedings that made the state possible. On June 20, 1863, West Virginia became the 35th state. That same day, the Restored Government of Virginia and its Governor Francis Pierpont vacated the Custom House and moved to Alexandria, Virginia. West Virginia's first Governor, Arthur Boreman, took up residency in the second floor offices once used by Pierpont and remained there until April 1864. The legislature moved to the Linsly Institute Building that still stands today on the northwest corner of Eoff Street and 15th Street.

Following West Virginia statehood, the Custom House returned to federal service until 1907 when a new federal building was built in Wheeling and the Custom House was sold. In 1963, in honor of the state's centennial, West Virginia purchased the Custom House and renamed it West Virginia Independence. In the years hence the building has been painstakingly restored and managed by the West Virginia Division of Culture and History. It stands today, restored to its original glory, and visitors can witness the stage upon which the Great State of West Virginia was created.

Visiting West Virginia Independence Hall

Today visitors to West Virginia Independence can see *West Virginia: Born of Civil War*, an exhibit feature period artifacts; *Waving for Liberty and Freedom*, a large collection of Civil War battles flags; the office used by Governor Francis Pierpont and the Surveyor of Customs; and the Wheeling room, dedicated to Wheeling's prominence in the 19th Century. On the third floor of the Custom House visitors can see the court room that has recently had its period murals, called trompe l'oeil, restored to its Civil War-era appearance. West Virginia Independence Hall is located at 1528 Market Street in Wheeling.

5

The Glory of the Golden Horseshoe[5]

It is a rich yellow hue, inscribed, and valued much more than its small size might imply. Once bejeweled, it evokes images of knights, ladies, honor, and glory; indeed possessing it is a privilege accorded to only a small percentage of West Virginians.

What is this extraordinary item? Any eighth grader in the Mountain State will tell you: It is the Golden Horseshoe, the symbolic golden pin possessed only by the elite members of the Golden Horseshoe Society. Since 1931, when 87 students from 46 counties were dubbed Knights and Ladies of the Golden Horseshoe, entrance to this distinguished society has been attempted by many but achieved by relatively few. Those who claim membership have exhibited exemplary knowledge of all aspects of West Virginia.

The origin of the Golden Horseshoe pin dates to 1716, the year Royal Lieutenant Governor Alexander Spotswood organized a 50-

---

[5] *A version of this article appeared in the May 2013 issue of* Wonderful West Virginia *Magazine.*

member party to cross the Allegheny Mountains. In Spotswood's day, the Blue Ridge marked the very line beyond which almost nothing was known. On September 5, Spotswood and his party—which included gentlemen, American Indian guides, soldiers, and slaves—looked across the Allegheny Mountains into the beautiful foothills and valleys westward. They were the first Europeans to see what is now central West Virginia. Drinking a toast to the health of King George I, they formally took possession of these new lands and fired a volley in celebration. They then explored the region and returned home to Williamsburg, Virginia's capital at the time.

To recognize their commitment and valor, Spotswood declared the men in his party "Knights of the Golden Horseshoe" and bestowed on each the gift of a small, gold horseshoe pin. Some of the pins were studded with precious gems and all bore the Latin inscription "Sic jurat transcendre montes," or "Thus he swears to cross the mountains." Today the same inscription graces the reverse side of the Golden Horseshoe pin sought by middle school students.

Only one of the original pins—encrusted with sapphires and diamonds—is known to still exist. Some researchers suggest that many pins were melted down during the Civil War.

Spotswood bestowed the pins hoping to inspire others to emigrate across the Blue Ridge Mountains and establish settlements on the land beyond. His gesture was politically savvy, as it associated travel west with the romance of Arthurian legend. Spotswood, who fought against the French in the Battle of Blenheim, wanted to extend English territory as much as possible. He was determined to expand the western frontier of Virginia and thereby prevent the French from doing so.

Some of the romantic traditions inspired by Lt Gov. Spotswood have transferred to today's Golden Horseshoe Award. Since 1931, winners of the award have knelt before the state superintendent of schools, who uses an antique sword to dub the students as Knights and Ladies of the Golden Horseshoe.

The Golden Horseshoe test was the brainchild of Phil Conely a historian, author, and the editor of the West Virginia Review at that time. In 1929, he pitched what he called "West Virginia Clubs" to William C. Cooke, then the state superintendent of schools. Conely wanted to persuade school students to think more about West Virginia history. The clubs encouraged fifth graders to become "Discoverers," sixth graders "Explorers," and seventh graders "Pioneers." In the eighth grade, students became "Junior Citizens" who were then eligible to compete for the Golden Horseshoe.

Cooke agreed, and thus began the nation's longest-running program of its kind. In 1931, more than 2,700 clubs with more than 48,000 members existed statewide. That year, the first induction ceremony was held in Charleston. Since then, 15,000 students have earned the Golden Horseshoe by passing the examination. (A searchable database of all past winners is available at the West Virginia Division of Culture and History website: http://www.wvculture.org/history/wvmemory/goldenhorseshoe.html).

Since 1975, an additional 189 adult recipients, including Gov. Jay Rockefeller; A. James Manchin; and Jim Comstock, beloved editor of the *West Virginia Hillbilly*, have all been named Honorary Golden Horseshoe winners. Nominated by county superintendents, honorary members must have made an outstanding contribution to West Virginia, West Virginia studies, and/or the Golden Horseshoe program.

The Golden Horseshoe test has always been highly challenging, one many adult West Virginians could not pass. The 1955 test consisted of four pages, single-spaced, and included a variety of question formats: multiple choice, completion, true/false, matching, short answer, and map identification. Topics covered were history, places of interest, West Virginia government, nature study and conservation, famous West Virginians, geography, and county identification. One section required test takers to "write a brief phrase to show why each of the following is of historic interest: Malden, Grave Creek Mound, Tu-Endie-Wei, Jackson's

Mill, Philippi, Seneca Trail, Fort Henry, Bunker Hill (WV)." Intimate knowledge of all things West Virginian was (and still is) essential.

Today, 221 Golden Horseshoe winners are selected each year. Each of the 55 counties has a minimum of two winners, and one winner is selected from each of the West Virginia Schools for the Deaf and Blind. The remaining winners are selected based on the populations of eighth graders in each of the counties.

Although it is a test, the event is also a competition. Students win by doing better than competing students in their county. Indeed, that number is profound. Every eighth grader in the state is eligible and many counties require all eighth graders to compete.

Today's test is taken online and consists of 45 to 50 multiple-choice questions. Some are knowledge-based recall questions and others are analytical questions, which might require students to read maps or analyze a speech. Today's Golden Horseshoe aspirant also writes an essay that typically traces some aspect of West Virginia though its history and impact. Essays are submitted to the West Virginia Department of Education, but are only used in tie-breaking situations.

Although an esteemed tradition in the Mountain State, the Golden Horseshoe Award has not been entirely without controversy. Before 1953, the award was given to African American students separately. The original rules allowed for four winners per county: "three whites and one Negro."

But even after school desegregation in 1955, trouble persisted. Paul "Rocky" Gates, the older brother of renowned author, Harvard University professor, and Mineral County native Henry Louis "Skip" Gates Jr., was a winner in 1957. Regrettably, Rocky Gates could not receive the award because he could not stay at the segregated hotel in Charleston where the winners stayed. This indignity was compounded by a lie when he was told by local officials, trying to spare his feelings, that he had misspelled a word and failed the test by a half point.

Rocky Gates did learn the truth and many years later, his

brother, Henry, arranged for his brother Rocky to receive the award on his 35th birthday, along with an apology from the governor. A few years later, when Henry Louis Gates Jr. was named the 1994 West Virginian of the Year by the Charleston Gazette, the State Senate passed a resolution recognizing his achievements and condemning the "vestiges of racial segregation that prevented his brother, Paul "Rocky" Gates, from receiving appropriate recognition as a 1957 Golden Horseshoe Award Winner."

A Golden Horseshoe winner in 1964, Henry Louis Gates, Jr. once referred to it as the "Nobel prize of eighth graders." Rocket Boys author Homer Hickam reported to State Department of Education officials that his one regret was not winning the Golden Horseshoe as a student. Hickam received the Honorary Golden Horseshoe Award in 1999. The rest of the original Rocket Boys received it in 2012.

As in past years, to be a Golden Horseshoe winner today requires dedicated study of all things West Virginian. Students must answer questions like these: Who was the West Virginian who ran for president in 1932 on the Liberty Party ticket and believed in the free coinage of silver? Of what material is the governor's mansion constructed? The rivalry between the football teams of West Virginia University and the University of Pittsburgh began in what year? In what Kanawha County community did Booker T. Washington spend his childhood? (*See below for answers.*)

The West Virginia Division of Culture and History website has about 2,000 sample questions to help students prepare for the test. The site had more than four million hits last year as students prepared for the Golden Horseshoe test and another challenge, the West Virginia History Bowl, a team game played with buzzers. Both contests require serious commitment and hours of study and practice. For the Golden Horseshoe especially, students desiring to win must make a plan and begin studying months or even years ahead of the big test day. Only the steadfast pursuit of knowledge can lead to entry into the lofty Golden Horseshoe Society and the glory of the gold.

Answers: William Hope "Coin" Harvey, brick, 1895, and Malden.

6

John F. Kennedy, Hubert Humphrey and the Battle for the 1960 West Virginia Presidential Primary[6]

Introduction

On May 10, 1960, the eyes of an anxious nation watched as the voters in West Virginia went to the polls. In the four weeks that made up the West Virginia primary in 1960, candidates, their families, friends and supporters logged hundreds of miles as they visited every corner of West Virginia in an effort to gather any and every vote. When the dust settled from the election West Virginia had changed the political landscape and altered conventional political wisdom.

---

[6] This article appeared in an *online exhibit produced by the West Virginia Archives and History Section on the West Virginia Division of Culture and History entitled: Battleground West Virginia: Electing the President in 1960. To access the website go to:*
http://www.wvculture.org/history/1960presidentialcampaign/1960presidentialcampaign.html

The general election in the fall became one of the closest presidential elections in United States history. On Election Day candidates and voters, alike, waited in anticipation until the wee hours of the following morning to see who was going to become the President of the United States.

Eyeing the White House

Presidential ambitions do not begin with the candidate standing before well-wishers announcing his or her candidacy. They begin months, years and even decades before that celebrated day. For presidential hopefuls, the election year of 1960 marked a golden opportunity to run for president. With the passage of the 22nd Amendment to the U.S. Constitution in 1951, Dwight Eisenhower became the first president of the United States to be limited by law to two four-year terms. Because of that change, both parties would be fielding new candidates. The early favorites of the Republican Party were Vice President Richard Nixon and New York Governor Nelson Rockefeller. In contrast, the Democratic Party was especially eager to avenge the landside defeats in the two previous presidential elections and regain the White House, which left the field full of possibilities as the party searched for a nominee who could win in the general election.

The Democratic National Convention in 1956 set the stage for the candidates who eventually made up the presidential field in 1960. During that convention, Adlai Stevenson received the party's presidential nomination for a second time, but in a move that defied tradition, he relinquished the responsibility of choosing his vice presidential candidate to the convention. In the wake of his decision, three men began to mobilize their forces to secure the coveted stepping-stone position of vice president: Massachusetts Senator John F. Kennedy, who placed Stevenson's name before the convention only days before; loyal supporter Minnesota Senator Hubert H. Humphrey; and Stevenson's main Democratic rival in

1952 and 1956, Tennessee Senator Estes Kefauver. Following two closely-contested ballots Kefauver out-distanced Kennedy and received the party's 1956 nomination for vice president.

Kennedy and his team realized that he lacked a national following and the political network necessary to secure a nomination at any future Democratic National Convention. To bolster his national appeal and to develop a political network, Kennedy made numerous trips across the United States to attend Democratic meetings, fundraising events, and gatherings, all in the hope of making important connections that he would need when election time came around in 1960. In spite of his defeat, Kennedy wasted little time and quickly joined the Democratic fight in 1956. On one of his stops Kennedy visited Wheeling on October 14, 1956, to speak on behalf of Adlai Stevenson at the Virginia Theatre. On this visit—his first to West Virginia--Kennedy spoke before a capacity crowd. In his speech entitled "The Problems of This Day," Kennedy argued that instead of a pathway to the future, Eisenhower and the Republicans were leading America on a "pathway of weakness." He furthered his comments with a verbal jab at then Vice President Nixon when he said the future of the Republican Party was the party of Nixon, and he believed that voters would reject a future with Nixon on Election Day. He also told the crowd that he believed that the race between Eisenhower and Stevenson was going to be a close one. While he thrilled the crowd with his speech, his pronouncement that the country would reject Eisenhower and Nixon and that the race was going to be close proved to be quite incorrect. Following his Virginia Theatre speech, the Massachusetts senator made an appearance at a rally held at Wheeling Park by the Holy Name Society, a united group of Catholic churches and organizations in the Ohio Valley. Newspaper coverage of his visit made no mention of Kennedy's religious affiliation and described his meeting with Catholic leaders in Wheeling as a meeting between friends. Four years later, Kennedy's religion would receive much greater attention and coverage in the campaign.

After his disappointing bid for the vice presidential nomination at the Democratic National Convention in 1956, Hubert Humphrey realized that to achieve his ambitions he would also have to raise his profile nationally and make more political connections. In the ensuing years, he made a widely publicized visit to meet Russian leader Nikita Khrushchev in 1958. Later in the year and in the weeks leading up to the 1958 congressional midterm elections, Humphrey made a trip to Moundsville to be the guest speaker at the Marshall County Democratic Dinner on October 4th. He further advanced his national appeal when he graced the cover of Time magazine in November following the Democratic congressional sweep of 1958 that sent West Virginia's Jennings Randolph and Robert C. Byrd to the U.S. Senate.

Kennedy also made the rounds supporting candidates in the 1958 midterm elections. He made his second trip to West Virginia on June 11, 1958, to make connections in the state's Democratic Party when he spoke to the party's fundraising Jefferson-Jackson Dinner in Morgantown. On October 9, and a few weeks before the 1958 midterm elections he made a return visit to the state when he visited the party faithful at Parkersburg to take part in a parade for Democrats. The following day Vice President Richard Nixon made a campaign stop in Huntington to bolster Republican support in the state.

While President Eisenhower was still very popular, the midterm elections of 1958 signaled big problems for Republicans. The election was a monumental victory for Democrats, who gained 16 seats in the Senate and 48 seats in the House of Representatives. With this tidal wave of success, the Democratic presidential hopefuls stepped up their travel schedules and made several high-profile trips to West Virginia.

Hubert Humphrey was the first presidential hopeful to return to West Virginia in 1959. On his visit he was the guest speaker at the 2nd Annual Democratic Women's Day banquet on March 21 at the Daniel Boone Hotel in Charleston. At the event he blasted the Eisenhower Administration for its lack of concern for people, saying that the administration "puts dollars before people, puts balancing the budget before balancing the nation's economy and puts fat corporate profits before full employment." On another visit on November 21, Humphrey spoke to approximately 400 people at a fundraising dinner for the Young Democrats of Raleigh County and the Raleigh County Democratic Executive Committee at the Beckley Hotel Ballroom.

To continue his efforts at widening his name recognition and popularity, John Kennedy returned to West Virginia on several key swing visits. In May, Kennedy visited southern West Virginia with Senator Jennings Randolph. Following a tour of the coal fields Kennedy made his way to Welch, where he was the guest speaker for the 75th Harry Truman Birthday Party held by Democrats in Mercer and McDowell counties. The following day he attended a rally held by the Democratic Party of Wyoming County. In October, Kennedy and his wife Jacqueline made a sweep through the state with well-publicized stops in Wellsburg and Charleston.

While the nomination for the Democratic Party seemed wide open in the fall of 1959, the Republican field was not as crowded, with only two serious candidates in line for the GOP nomination. Vice President Richard Nixon was the front runner for the nomination and was playing the role as the heir apparent to the White House. Nixon's only viable rival for the nomination was the newly elected New York Governor Nelson Rockefeller. Unlike the complex coalition of the Democratic Party, the Republican Party in the late 1950s was formed by two differing factions: a progressive, moralistic and reform-minded faction of the Teddy Roosevelt mold and a fiscally conservative pro-business faction. In an effort to measure the political lay of the land, Rockefeller and his political team traveled the country from early October to December to meet with the key financial supporters and power brokers of the Republican Party to gauge support for his bid for the White House. When Rockefeller and his team met in late December of 1959, it was clear to them that the business wing of the party wanted Nixon and would financially support only him.

What many of Nixon's rivals failed to recognize was the political positioning Nixon was accomplishing from the Vice Presidency. While many believed that the role of vice president was only a position of glad-handing, ribbon cuttings and parades, Nixon used these opportunities during his eight-year tenure as vice president to meet with the key supporters of the party, forge close relationships and most importantly lock up their financial support for his presidential run in 1960. Faced with this reality, the Rockefeller team realized that any run without support from the party's financial wing was doomed to failure. Rockefeller quietly bowed out as he boarded a train for the Christmas holiday. For the Nixon camp, the Rockefeller withdrawal was a huge disappointment because Nixon and his advisors believed that the primary fight would provide an opportunity to enliven the party and keep his name before voters. With Rockefeller out of the picture, Nixon had to be content on sidelines while Democrats in their primary battles continually bashed Republicans, the Eisenhower Administration, and the Vice President. Nixon and his advisors feared that the unchecked attacks would undermined the major component of his appeal to voters. The Nixon team also realized that his message would be lost during the primary season because without a primary opponent to battle, the press would not seek him out, and Democrats would dominate press coverage from January until the Democratic National Convention in July. Nixon was left trying to garner positive attention while he waited for the general election campaign to begin in earnest in the fall.

Primary Preparations and Strategies

When the presidential primary season began most campaign watchers gave little thought to West Virginia. Only Senator Hubert H. Humphrey of Minnesota and Senator John F. Kennedy of Massachusetts were officially on the West Virginia ballot for president, but other contenders for the office, like Senate Majority Leader Lyndon B. Johnson and Missouri Senator Stuart Symington, were aggressively working behind the scenes to further their own political ambitions. Johnson and Symington were working to derail Kennedy's bid for the nomination by prolonging the primary fight between Kennedy and Humphrey in hopes that a deadlocked Democratic convention would seek a compromise candidate on a second or third ballot. Johnson believed that his political clout and senatorial connections could mobilize support to push him over the top. Symington believed that his defense experience and the political weight and support of fellow Missourian and former President Harry S. Truman could convince delegates at the convention to support him.

While the Democratic field was crowded with ambitious upstarts and connected power brokers, the biggest and most prominent unknown of the campaign was former Illinois Governor Adlai Stevenson. Stevenson had twice run unsuccessfully for the presidency in 1952 and 1956 with landslide losses to the Republican Dwight Eisenhower. In spite of these major losses, Stevenson was still politically prominent and remained a favorite of the liberal wing of the Democratic Party which included one of his biggest supporters, former First Lady Eleanor Roosevelt. In 1952 Democratic leaders had drafted Stevenson into the presidential nomination at the convention, and many believed, and hoped, that if the door was left open he could be drafted again in 1960. Stevenson, himself, made little effort to promote that scenario, but he also made little effort to close that door either, and many political observers believe that he was still interested in the office.

In the summer of 1959, Kennedy and Humphrey were both honing their strategy to obtain the Democratic nomination. In total there were 16 states in 1960 that were holding primary elections to determine representation to the Democratic National Convention in Los Angeles. The Kennedy camp viewed Wisconsin as the state where victory could eliminate Humphrey, who they saw as his main competition in the primaries. Kennedy's camp hoped that the primaries would reveal that Humphrey's political appeal was weak and limited only to Minnesota. Kennedy also believed that a strong showing in the primaries would convince political bosses in the East that he was a serious candidate who could deliver the presidency to the Democratic Party.

The Humphrey camp, planning in Minnesota during the summer of 1959, believed that his hopes rested on the 5 primaries that would most likely support his candidacy: Wisconsin, the District of Columbia, West Virginia, Oregon, and South Dakota. With a victory in Wisconsin he believed that he could raise enough money to contend in West Virginia, and with each subsequent victory more money would become available. If he could last, and with help at the convention, Humphrey believed that he could receive the nomination and defeat Nixon in November.

In hopes of getting a jump on the Kennedy campaign, Humphrey formally announced his candidacy for president on December 30, 1959. Kennedy followed a few days later when he formally announced his candidacy January 2, 1960. For the next few months the other candidates remained on the sidelines. The first to move from the shadows was Symington, who in an effort to put his name before the public before the Wisconsin primary, announced his candidacy on March 24. Johnson never formally announced, but his closely tied supporters announced an "unofficial" Johnson for President Committee as early as October of 1959. While he wasn't officially in the race, he, along with Adlai Stevenson, was a part of any serious discussion of the Democratic nomination.

With the campaign officially underway, Humphrey was the first candidate to stop in West Virginia. In late January of 1960, Humphrey spoke before the West Virginia House of Delegates. During his speech, Humphrey declared that poverty was an issue that undermined the country's national strength and that the Eisenhower Administration stood like a "stunned ox . . . unwilling and unable apparently to understand what is going on." Also during the speech he addressed issues that found a willing audience in the State Capitol when he called for the expansion of federally sponsored research to find additional uses for the state's abundant natural resources and for steps to end the cut-rate practices of foreign countries in the coal market.

Although both Kennedy and Humphrey had announced their candidacy neither candidate had officially filed the paperwork to enter the West Virginia Primary. On February 3, 1960, however, that changed when the Humphrey campaign announced that he was going to formally enter the West Virginia primary. That same day the Kennedy campaign called a press conference at the West Virginia Secretary of State's office in Charleston. The campaign later retracted their statement and announced that the press conference would instead take place in Washington because Kennedy had legislative duties in the Senate that would prevent him from making the trip on the 4th. In the wee hours of October 6, Kennedy did make the trip to Charleston to formally file his primary paperwork and to provide a press conference from Secretary of State Joe Burdette's office. Following the brief visit Kennedy boarded a plane and flew to his next speaking engagement in the west.

The first primary election on the 1960 election calendar was held on March 8 in New Hampshire. Kennedy was the only serious contender on the ballot. Humphrey steered clear of the contest because he realized that Kennedy's political strength was in New England and participation in the primary would result in a humiliating second place finish. When the votes were counted Kennedy won by a huge margin, even doubling the previous primary record held by Estes Kefauver in 1956. While the victory did not change the minds of powerbrokers in the Democratic Party who questioned the viability of his candidacy, Kennedy must have relished eclipsing the vote total record held by Kefauver, who four years earlier nudged him from the vice presidential nomination at the Democratic Convention. In spite of the victory, everyone who followed politics knew that the first real test for Kennedy and Humphrey was Wisconsin.

On March 16, Kennedy returned to West Virginia to open his campaign headquarters at the Kanawha Hotel in Charleston.

During the press conference Kennedy told reporters that he believed West Virginians were more concerned with economic issues than with his religion. He answered questions about Missouri Senator Stuart Symington, who was speaking before the Third Annual Democratic Women's Day luncheon on the following Saturday. Kennedy told reporters that he wished Symington would have run in the primaries because they were an important part of the process. He explained that the hopes of Johnson and Symington rested with Hubert Humphrey, a prolonged primary battle, and a hung convention. Kennedy further explained that he believed that the voters of West Virginia would choose between Humphrey and himself, and that he wouldn't be part of any scheme devised by Symington or Johnson.

A few days later on March 19, Symington spoke before the Democratic Women's Day luncheon in Charleston. Unlike Hubert Humphrey, who spoke before the group the year before, Symington didn't have the event solely to himself. Also attending and representing Humphrey was his sister Mrs. Frances Howard of Baltimore, while Kennedy was represented by his brother Ted. Symington was coy with reporters about announcing his candidacy, but most in the crowd knew he was interested in being president. In political circles Symington was dubbed the "Missouri Compromise" for the Democratic nomination. Before the crowd of 500, Symington made it known that he was becoming "more interested" in running for president. Presenting a humble posture, he told the crowd that it was because of the urgings of the people who he met in his travels and letter writers who shared with the senator their apprehensive outlook of the future. In an interview with Gazette-Mail reporter Mary Chilton Abbot, Symington dropped his coy stance and admitted that he would accept the nomination if offered. Following his visit Symington must have become even more interested in the office because a few days later, on March 24, he formally announced his candidacy.

On the heels of Kennedy and Symington, Humphrey made a visit to Huntington on March 23 to address a crowd of about 300

Democrats at the Hotel Frederick. Humphrey was three hours late for the engagement because he was tending to Senate business. During his speech Humphrey was quick to blame the state's and the country's economic woes directly on the Eisenhower Administration and its policies, but he was careful not to place blame on Eisenhower the man for fear of offending voters who had elected him twice. In closing, he urged voters to support Jennings Randolph in his reelection bid for a full 6-year Senate term against sitting Governor Cecil Underwood. He also urged voters to support Congressman Ken Hechler in his bid to return to the House of Representatives. Following his speech Humphrey boarded a plane for his return to Washington.

The Wisconsin Primary

It was fitting that the first major showdown between Humphrey and Kennedy took place in Wisconsin, the state where the primary election took the selection of candidates from political bosses in the cigar-filled backrooms to the daylight of the ballot box and the hands of the people. In fact, primaries as a concept were first launched in Wisconsin in 1903 under the leadership of congressman, governor, senator, and Progressive Party presidential candidate Robert LaFollette. Primaries quickly spread to other states, and today they are the preferred method of most states. In spite of their ability to keep elections close to the people and democratic, primaries are brutal, messy, and expensive affairs that often turn friends to foes and rip political parties asunder while they are trying to conserve resources for the general election fight. For the ambitious who seek the presidency, however, the primary is a necessary evil. To gain the delegates needed to carry the convention, candidates must crisscross states in the hopes of convincing more and more people to support their cause.

In 1960 Wisconsin had 31 delegates up for grabs. Ten of those delegates would be determined by a winner-take-all statewide vote. Each of the state's 10 congressional districts would choose 2 delegates. The choice of the final delegate was to be split by the party's national committeeman and national committeewoman. With the stage set, both Kennedy and Humphrey poured all of their energy and a reported sum of $150,000 each into Wisconsin. Later reports showed that Humphrey spent in the neighborhood of $116,500, while spending by the Kennedy camp was substantially more than reported in the press.

As the campaign heated up in Wisconsin, Humphrey crisscrossed the state in a rented tour bus. Kennedy, his family, Harvard friends and war buddies visited towns, hamlets, and farm communities across the dairy state. As Election Day neared, Kennedy, confident of his chances against Humphrey, boasted to the press that if he lost in Wisconsin he was out of the race. Kennedy's hope was that with defeat Humphrey would do the same and leave him the only candidate crossing the country collecting delegates for the convention in Los Angeles. Humphrey, however, would not return the boast and battled on to the Primary Election Day. As results came in the Kennedy camp was confident of victory, but they kept a watchful eye on four of Wisconsin's ten voting districts. The second, third, ninth and tenth districts were predominantly Protestant and three of them were rural in nature. With victory in these non-Catholic areas Kennedy would put an end to the Catholic issue and would show that he could win as a national candidate in November. When the votes were finally counted, Kennedy defeated Humphrey by a total of 476,024 to 366,753. While Kennedy won 56% of the vote, had the highest vote total in Wisconsin history, and defeated Hubert Humphrey in his own backyard, many eyes focused on those Protestant voting districts that fell into the Humphrey column.

The prevailing view that Protestant America would not support a Catholic candidate continued to nag Kennedy and brought his entire campaign into doubt. In Wisconsin, the conventional wisdom forged in 1928 when Catholic presidential candidate Al Smith failed in his attempt to defeat Herbert Hoover was again supported by Kennedy's defeat in the Protestant districts.

Humphrey was emboldened by his stronger than expected showing which led he and his supporters to believe that, in spite of his campaign's financial woes, the results in West Virginia would be different. Kennedy, denied the knockout punch in Wisconsin, moved his troops to West Virginia to battle Humphrey again. Several key Democrats and union leaders urged Humphrey to bow out, but those with their eyes on the White House urged him to go on with the hopes that the Kennedy machine could be derailed.

On to West Virginia

With their families, friends, and dedicated volunteers, Kennedy and Humphrey embarked on a campaign the likes the United States had never before seen. During the month of April both campaigns cruised the cities, made stops in county seats, entertained rural hamlets, and scoured every hollow and hillside of the state to reach every last voter. All the while, other Democratic candidates waited in the wings and schemed in hopes of a prolonged campaign that would result in a deadlocked convention that would open the door for their own presidential ambitions.

Unlike Wisconsin, the 25 delegates to the 1960 Democratic National Convention from West Virginia were not bound by party rules to support the winner of the primary, which led many in the West Virginia press to refer derisively to the primary as nothing more than a popularity contest. For the candidates on the ballot, victory in West Virginia secured little in their quest for the nomination. At the national convention, delegates from the state could abandon the winner entirely and swing their support to his primary opponent or even to those who waited on the sidelines. In spite of the possibilities, Humphrey and Kennedy moved into West Virginia, both realizing the state was paramount to their success. For Humphrey a victory in West Virginia would revive his struggling campaign. For Kennedy the primary provided an opportunity not only to eliminate Humphrey, but also to prove that his presidential campaign could overcome the barriers that many believed would deliver the presidency to Nixon and the Republicans.

Members of the Kennedy team quickly made a night trip from Wisconsin following the election on the Caroline, a Convair turbo-prop plane purchased by Joe Kennedy and leased to his son's campaign, four weeks to the day remained until the West Virginia Primary on May 10. As Kennedy's brother Bobby and his national campaign director Larry O'Brien reached Clarksburg to assess the lay of the land and to meet with the northern chairmen at the Stonewall Jackson Hotel, they were faced with a new reality on the ground. Gallup polls from December had Kennedy winning West Virginia by a 70 to 30 margin, but as news of the campaign in Wisconsin reached the front pages of West Virginia's newspapers, the polls were revealing that Kennedy's lead had not only evaporated, but Humphrey had a 60 to 40 advantage. After a meeting in Clarksburg, Bobby and O'Brien made their way to the Kanawha Hotel in Charleston to meet with their southern chairmen. In a frank and heated meeting it was revealed to the Kennedy team that the religion issue had become front and center in the campaign and with it the tide had turned. From Charleston, Bobby shared the drastic turn of events with Kennedy in Washington and then he made a quick return to Washington to strategize.

Senator Hubert Humphrey was the first candidate to arrive in the state, touching down in Charleston at 1:00 a.m. on April 8 following a flight from Washington. After three hours of sleep, the Minnesota senator climbed aboard his campaign bus and started on a 77-mile trip that would include 16 stops and eventually end in Beckley. His first stop on the trip was to visit workers on their way to work at the Libbey-Owens glass factory in Kanawha City. He made a side trip up Cabin Creek before stopping for lunch in Montgomery. At Beckley, Humphrey spoke before the Memorial Building where he linked Vice President Nixon and the "veto, go-slow, no-go" Eisenhower Administration record. On Saturday, April 9th, Humphrey visited Hinton, Princeton, Madison, and

Charleston where Humphrey flew to Washington for a television appearance on Sunday, April 10. He returned to Charleston on that same day to speak in place of his sister who was scheduled to speak at the Kanawha Valley Unitarian Fellowship. On Monday, April 11, Humphrey again hit the road making another trip through the southern coalfields with stops in Logan, Williamson, Welch and Bluefield; but on this trip, he would not have the state to himself as Kennedy made his way to Parkersburg.

On April 11, Kennedy and his team flew into Parkersburg to have coffee and to attend a rally. Following the rally, Kennedy flew to Charleston where he spoke at Morris Harvey College (now the University of Charleston) to a large crowd. After lunch the senator drove to Huntington where he spoke from the hood of a car near the Marshall campus and then flew to Beckley to speak to a crowd of 500 in front of the Raleigh County Courthouse. Kennedy's busy day ended in Beckley.

Kennedy's presence in West Virginia marked a dramatic change in the tone of the campaign discourse. On April 11, recently-elected Senator Robert C. Byrd announced in an interview that he was supporting Hubert Humphrey and encouraged others in West Virginia to do the same. Byrd stated that Humphrey was not his first choice for president, which was Lyndon Johnson, who he felt was best qualified, followed by Stuart Symington. He explained that Humphrey would be his choice for vice president, and that he felt Kennedy was too young and inexperienced to be president. He encouraged other supporters of Johnson, Symington and Adlai Stevenson to vote for Humphrey to derail Kennedy's campaign. In speeches following Byrd's pronouncement, Kennedy derided the organized campaign that was being carried out against him. Humphrey, in response to a reporter's question about Kennedy's charges that there was an organized Stop Kennedy campaign, quipped "Poor Little Jack!" and continued with, "I wish he would grow up and stop acting like a boy."

While the forces appeared to be lining up against Kennedy, he had an opportunity to address what was becoming the major issue of the primary directly. After his April 11th, stop at Morris Harvey College, Kennedy responded to a question about his religion, saying, "There is nothing in my religious faith that prevents me from executing my oath of office. If I thought there was I wouldn't have taken it. If I thought there was I shouldn't be a candidate for president. If I thought there was I shouldn't be a senator. I shouldn't have been a congressman and, to be frank, I shouldn't have been taken into the service of the United States." With that, the religion issue moved from the periphery of the Kennedy campaign to center stage with his next tour of the state a week later.

Beginning in Charleston on April 18, Muriel Humphrey, the candidate's wife, and their two sons Bob and Douglas joined the campaign in West Virginia. The group began what the press called "the station wagon campaign" with stops at grocery stores, filling stations, garages, and country stores in Clendenin, Sutton, and Buckhannon before arriving in Clarksburg. As she spoke with voters she also passed out a recipe for beef soup that had become a part of the campaign in Wisconsin. In the evening Mrs. Humphrey and her sons arrived to meet with 300 well-wishers who were attending the grand opening of Humphrey's Clarksburg campaign headquarters. On the following day Mrs. Humphrey and her sons continued the tour with stops in Bridgeport, Grafton, and Morgantown.

When Kennedy returned to the state on April 18, he set out on a three-day tour of the Catholic portions of the state in north-central West Virginia and the state's northern panhandle. Following his visits to Clarksburg and Fairmont, Kennedy and his wife Jacqueline toured Osage and Scotts Run before attending a reception at the Hotel Morgan in Morgantown. The Kennedys then boarded their campaign plane and headed to the Wheeling-Ohio County Airport where they landed at 10:41 p.m. On the following morning Kennedy traveled to Bethany. Responding directly to a heckler in the crowd who asked him how he could reconcile being president with being Catholic, Kennedy said, "I don't take orders from above," and followed with "I am going to any church where I want, regardless of whether I am elected president or not!" Following his stop at Bethany, he continued on to West Liberty State College before returning to Wheeling where he made visits to the Sylvania Electric Products and the Hazel-Atlas plants before departing for Beckley. The final day of his tour started in Beckley with Kennedy making stops in Fayetteville, Mt. Hope, Gauley Bridge, Montgomery, Charleston, and ending the day at the Pritchard Hotel in Huntington.

The next day, April 21, Kennedy took the religion issue to a national audience when he spoke before the American Society of Newspaper Editors in Washington D.C. In a speech entitled, "The Religion Issue in American Politics" Kennedy confronted all of the religion talk that was being reported about his campaign and discussed by political commentators. Kennedy chastised the press for obsessing about religion, religious bigotry and the suggested Catholic voting bloc, instead of the other issues in the campaign. He expressed the hope that the press would stop referring to him as the "Catholic candidate." In closing, he acknowledged that with this campaign it was his task to directly address the legitimate concerns of voters in the campaign, but he also offered that the task of the press was "to refute falsehood, to inform the ignorant, and to concentrate on the issues, the real issues, in this hour of the nation's peril."

While Kennedy was busy addressing religion in northern West Virginia and Washington, His brothers Bobby and Ted, and former Congressman Franklin Roosevelt, Jr., were making stops on behalf of the campaign. Humphrey, also absent from the political scene in West Virginia, had his wife and sons, along with Minnesota Lieutenant Governor Karl Rolvaag. Also making stops for Humphrey were Congressmen Charles Porter of Oregon and Joseph Karth of Minnesota, Senator Eugene McCarthy of Minnesota, Minnesota Governor Orville Freeman, Wisconsin Lieutenant Governor Philleo Nash and former ambassador to Denmark Eugenie Anderson. Humphrey's sister Frances Howard also made visits on his behalf.

On April 25, Kennedy returned to the state and began a planned three-day swing through the coalfields of southern West Virginia. He began his visit in Huntington and headed for Wayne, Williamson, and Logan. An hour before Kennedy's arrival in Wayne, David Brinkley of NBC's Huntley-Brinkley Report set up cameras to record his speech for a national television audience. Kennedy spoke before a crowd of 250 onlookers in Wayne and took the time to shake the hands with all who had gathered. The following evening Brinkley's footage ran on his television show and caused a stir with his description of Wayne and the Wayne Bridge that he called "the noisiest anywhere." The story on the Huntley-Brinkley Report created a fervor when Governor Cecil Underwood in response to the story lashed out at Brinkley and his coverage in the local press. The governor also took his concerns to the Federal Communications Commission and appealed for the commission to take action. Chairman Frederick W. Ford responded that to him it appeared that Brinkley did not make a "sufficient effort to balance the unfavorable comment on West Virginia," but that there was little to warrant any action by the FCC. Prior to Brinkley's reports from Wayne and Mercer County, Republicans in West Virginia remained relatively quiet observers of the Democratic contest, but in a sudden change of tactics they demanded that Kennedy and Humphrey stop slandering the state. Others in the Republican camp invited both candidates to pack up and leave the state. For the residents of Wayne, good news came from the ordeal when the West Virginia State Road Commission began "previously scheduled maintenance" to replace the decking on the bridge on May 6.

On April 26, Kennedy visited Bluefield State College, Bramwell, Mullens and Princeton. During a visit with miners near Itmann, Kennedy almost faced a serious accident when he strayed too close to high voltage electric wires used to power coal cars. Luckily, for him 200 miners getting off their shift shouted a warning in time to prevent any harm. On the third day of his swing through the southern coal fields, Kennedy was forced to cut his trip short when he flew back to Washington to vote on a mine safety bill that was pending in the Senate.

Following Kennedy's departure, the Kennedy campaign experienced a rare political gaff brought on by the weather. Because of the change of plans and bad weather that prevented his brother Ted from landing and attending the rally, the Kennedy bus arrived in Hinton without anyone to speak to the disappointed crowd of 600 people who had been waiting for Kennedy in the rain. The Bluefield Daily Telegraph described the pitiful scene and quoted a bystander who said the whole thing was a "Pretty darned awkward situation." Kennedy promised a return visit to Hinton on May 4, but the folks in Hinton were let down again two days later when FDR, Jr. failed to appear at a rally held in the McCreery Hotel. In his absence, Senator Robert Byrd co-opted the event and urged the crowd to support his candidacy as a delegate to the Democratic National Convention and to remind them that he supported Hubert Humphrey in the primary.

Humphrey returned to Charleston on Sunday night April 24 for more campaigning. On the following morning he left Charleston at 6:00 am. During the day his campaign bus made visits to Summersville, Craigsville, Webster Springs, Buckhannon, Philippi and Fairmont. At Summersville Humphrey said that Republicans had the "imagination of a crocodile" because they did not move power generation closer to the coal fields.

After the long trip Humphrey spoke before 200 people attending the $10-a-plate dinner held by the Marion County Democratic Committee at Fairmont. At the event, Humphrey called the Eisenhower Administration the most inept since the Grant Administration. He further railed against Eisenhower's veto of a coal research bill approved by Congress. Following the dinner, Humphrey admitted to a reporter's questions that his campaign funds were running low, but he assured them that he had enough to continue and, in an obvious slight toward Kennedy, he hoped that American politics would not be left exclusively to the rich and "peddled like hotdogs on the street."

On the 26th, Humphrey traveled from Fairmont to Grafton and made his way east on U.S. Route 50, stopping in Kingwood, Terra Alta, Keyser, Romney, Berkeley Springs, Martinsburg, and Charles Town. The trip got off to a rocky start when Humphrey and his team started late because they did not take Daylight Savings Time into account. Humphrey, however, motored on and continued a theme that he shared with reporters in Fairmont the previous night. At Kingwood, he changed his message from his brutal assault on the Eisenhower Administration and Republicans to one in which he lamented to voters that he was like them and that it would be sad if America was only run by the rich and the "pets of political bosses."

By the time the Humphrey entourage reached Keyser they had lost another hour and were two hours behind the published schedule. Crowds that had assembled to meet the senator at the published time dwindled, and by the end of the day, only diehards remained to greet him. Questions from reporters in Keyser received a heated response from Humphrey who bristled under the line of questions and accusations that were uttered on the campaign trail. In response to one reporter's question about Jimmy Hoffa providing money for his campaign Humphrey replied that he was tired of suggestions that he was being financed by Hoffa, Symington, or Johnson. He went on to say that he was also tired of every one of his criticisms of Kennedy being painted as religious bigotry by his opponent and his campaign. Humphrey ended his day by returning to Washington where on the following day he joined Kennedy in the Senate to vote in support of mine safety legislation that was pending.

Following the vote in the Senate, Humphrey returned to West Virginia and spent the entire day of April 28 in Charleston campaigning. At noon he started to speak to a crowd on Capitol Street, but the public address system failed. Unfazed, Humphrey delivered the speech with a portable loud speaker and laughing, asked the crowd, "I wondered if the Republicans arranged that." At 2:00 p.m. Humphrey spoke before a crowd at Morris Harvey and humor again smoothed over an awkward situation. When a student arose to ask a question, he erroneously addressed Humphrey as "Sen. Kennedy." Without missing a beat Humphrey told the crowd that it was okay because "100,000 people in Wisconsin made the same mistake." While humor marked the campaign trail that day Humphrey addressed serious issues. He criticized Republicans for their meager help to the poor and also said that Senator Kennedy was a good man, but that voters should look at his record and his experience. At Morris Harvey, he turned to foreign policy and Korea and told students that it was important to address poverty and hunger around the world because these conditions played into the hands of demagogues and Communists. On a television press conference that evening Humphrey continued his assault on Republicans, especially their programs for the poor.

As Election Day neared the niceties and the decorum of the campaign faded and the gloves came off. For the first time the candidates themselves began directly sparing with each other in the press. At a stop on Friday, April 29, Kennedy accused Humphrey of attacking his integrity and smearing his record. Humphrey, busy making stops in Huntington, Hamlin, Chapmanville, and Logan, first responded to Kennedy's accusation in Huntington with wonder, but by the time he reached Logan, Humphrey's strategy was to plead innocence and then to question Kennedy's maturity. After hearing about Humphrey's statements, Bobby Kennedy, speaking for his brother from the Charleston campaign office, released a statement that said that Kennedy would not respond because he believed that "no Democrat is ever going to win in 1960 by imitating Vice President Richard Nixon." This comment was followed up with a statement that Humphrey could not win the nomination, the election or become president of the United States. With that, the chorus of Kennedy supporters began to echo that statement and others that questioned Humphrey's chances for the nomination and his ability to defeat Nixon in the fall.

On the campaign trail, April 30 in Richwood proved to be one of the more colorful of the entire campaign. The day was marked in Richwood as Fishing Day, the opening of trout season on Summit Lake, and the community's Annual Ramp Dinner. The most awkward moment of the day occurred when FDR, Jr., and Humphrey encountered one another in the doorway of the Richwood Grade School, where the ramp dinner was being held.

The emerging nastiness of the campaign was displayed when campaign cars adorned with loud speakers, one following FDR, Jr., and representing Kennedy and another supporting Humphrey, exchanged words and tried to out squawk each other on Main Street. Order was restored when the town policeman arrived to settle the matter. By the end of the fracas, FDR, Jr., had had enough. To make matters worse for Roosevelt, he was forced to endure another encounter with the very same policeman that only a few weeks earlier had made headlines across the country when Roosevelt tried to use his clout and family name to bypass a funeral and the Richwood policeman retorted that he didn't care if he was Abraham Lincoln he wasn't getting through.

Roosevelt was also sore at Richwood Leader editor Jim Comstock who leaked the funeral story to the Associated Press and had written a satirical article for his spoof paper *The West Virginia Hillbilly* on religious prejudice called, "Pa Ain't Sellin' His Vote to No Catholic." While Roosevelt found the article particularly distasteful, a few reporters unfamiliar with *The West Virginia Hillbilly* and Comstock's widely-known sense of humor had quoted the article in out-of-state newspapers as proof of West Virginia's religious bigotry. Many papers later ran retractions, but others did not address the error. For the folks of Richwood and the surrounding area Fishing Day and the Annual Ramp Dinner proved to be banner events. The next edition of Comstock's *Times Leader* must have delighted subscribers when a picture of Humphrey's face as he had his first taste of ramps graced the pages of his newspaper.

The nastiness of the campaign also began to spread between parties. Republican Governor Cecil Underwood, still seething from David Brinkley's report from Wayne, stepped up his vocal criticism of Humphrey and Kennedy and their criticisms of Eisenhower and Republicans, especially when it related to West Virginia. In response to Underwood's comments Kennedy suggested that he knew West Virginia better than the governor and that both Eisenhower and Underwood's Republican administration had neglected West Virginia for far too long.

While the campaign rhetoric was growing louder, Kennedy's actual voice failed him. With only ten days remaining in the campaign, Kennedy was forced to begin what the press called his "whisper campaign." Kennedy's day began at Madison where approximately 200 people gathered to meet him on the lawn of the Boone County Courthouse. At Eskdale on Cabin Creek, Kennedy was relegated to shaking hands while Matt Reese of Huntington spoke to the crowd. During his speech Reese reminded the crowd of Kennedy's heroic military service and further pointed out that Kennedy was the only veteran in the race. In the evening Kennedy administrative assistant, Ted Sorenson, spoke for Kennedy during his visit to the Kanawha Valley Unitarian Fellowship and rallies at the City Auditorium in Nitro and the junior high school at St. Albans. During the evening he was joined by his wife Jackie who assured the crowd that she was providing "gargles and pills" for her husband. Following the rallies the Kennedy camp moved on to Parkersburg late in the evening.

On May 1, Kennedy hit the campaign trail with a visit to the Ravenswood Community Center where he met with a crowd of 1,200 people. Kennedy was still ailing from a throat infection and had turned speaking duties over to his brother Ted. Following Ravenswood, Kennedy moved on to Parkersburg to meet with a rally before attending an ox roast at the Parkersburg City Park. Again Ted took over the main speaking duties at the event, but Kennedy in his brief address explained to the crowd that the main reason he joined the Navy and ran for Congress and was the same reason he was running for president. It was, he said, because he was "brought up to have a strong devotion to [his] country." Following the ox roast Kennedy and Ted moved on to Weirton to speak before the Order of Italian Sons and Daughters of America. Kennedy addressed charges lodged by Governor Underwood that Teamster President Jimmy Hoffa was going to influence West Virginia's election. Kennedy doubted that the people of West Virginia would be influenced by Hoffa who had announced his support of Humphrey. Following the stop in Weirton, Kennedy took a day off from campaigning in the state.

Humphrey spent Sunday in Washington, D.C. to campaign for the primary held there on Tuesday, May 3. Returning to West Virginia on Monday, May 2, Humphrey touched down at 11:00 am and made a whirlwind tour of Parkersburg. He made scheduled meetings with local labor leaders and the local media outlets before meeting voters in the downtown. Humphrey spoke in front of the Wood County Courthouse where he stated that economic issues were the most important to West Virginia voters, but he lamented in an obvious jab at Kennedy and the press that it was difficult to get the message out when all that the press was concerned with was personalities and not a candidate's stand on the issues. Later that evening Humphrey spoke before 2,000 people at the local VFW hall. During his address he called for the need to plan for the future instead of continuing on the path that had created the poor economy. Following his address and meeting with the attendees Humphrey headed for Huntington where he had a full slate of events planned for the following day.

Humphrey spent May 3 in Huntington. The day began early with a visit to a local factory where workers were on strike. Refusing to cross the picket line, Humphrey moved on and visited another Huntington factory before returning to the Hotel Frederick to attend the Democratic Citizens Breakfast. Following the breakfast, Humphrey met with radio and television reporters at the hotel before attending a meeting with the local Kiwanis Club at noon. In the afternoon he hit the streets of Huntington before attending his largest gathering in West Virginia, Humphrey Day at Camden Park, where nearly 10,000 people took advantage of free rides at the park. Humphrey spoke to the crowd from the roof of an ice cream stand. Following the stop, Humphrey travelled to Charleston to take part in a televised debate with Kennedy.

Kennedy resumed his campaign on May 3 with an evening visit to Welch. At the McDowell County Courthouse Kennedy briefly spoke to an overcapacity crowd in the courtroom. The theme of his ten minute speech was that one of the biggest problems facing the next president was to figure out what to do with miners that had been replaced by automation in the coal industry. Following his brief words and a speech by his brother Ted, Kennedy stood in a doorway and shook the hand of everyone who came to hear him speak.

On May 4, Kennedy, his brother Ted, and FDR, Jr., began their day in Athens where they appeared at Concord College. Before a group of approximately 1,000 students and faculty members, Kennedy, in spite of his sore throat, roused the crowd when he told them that he was glad that Concord, Massachusetts, decided to name their town after the school. The crowd erupted again when he told the crowd that after traveling the state he truly understood the West Virginia motto that Mountaineers are Always Free.

Following the visit to Athens, Kennedy finally made good on a promise to visit Hinton. The special visit was scheduled to Hinton to make up for a series of missed visits by Kennedy, Ted, and FDR, Jr. Kennedy spoke to a crowd of 600 or 700 people from the back of a truck for only 6 minutes, when he was replaced by his brother who was then followed by FDR, Jr. Kennedy spoke about the economic issues of West Virginia, and the neglect that had befallen the parks, and the decline of the natural beauty and water quality of local rivers which hampered tourism efforts in the area. When Ted addressed the crowd, he assured them that if his brother won in West Virginia he would win the nomination, and then West Virginians would have a good friend in the White House. When FDR, Jr., spoke to those who had gathered near the Summers County Courthouse, he was blunt and to the point. The former congressman told the crowd that Hubert Humphrey was merely a "straw man" for those candidates who chose to avoid the West Virginia primary because they knew that they would have been soundly defeated. He further told the crowd that they had a clear choice: either throw their vote away on a straw man or support the next President of the United States. Following the speeches in Hinton, Kennedy moved on to Alderson where he briefly outlined his plan to attract industry to Greenbrier County before making his way to White Sulphur Springs.

Arriving there at 2:45 pm, Kennedy explained to the crowd that the election of 1960 was even more important than the election of 1932 that ushered in the New Deal. In an uncharacteristic move for Kennedy, he charged that Humphrey was distorting his record and "playing fast and loose with smears and innuendos." He went on to state that Humphrey simply could not win the nomination. Kennedy was careful to provide a list Humphrey's good qualities, but he lamented that, in spite of those qualities, Humphrey just couldn't win the nomination. Following the speech Kennedy made his way to Charleston where he would meet Humphrey in a televised debate that evening.

The May 4, Kennedy-Humphrey Debate was a joint project between the *Charleston Gazette* and a network of television stations across West Virginia: WCHS-TV, Charleston; WHIS-TV, Bluefield; WTRF-TV, Wheeling; WBOY-TV, Clarksburg; and WTAP-TV, Parkersburg. The televised debate, the first of its kind in the United States, was broadcast nationally by the Mutual Broadcasting Company. Television stations in New York, San Francisco, Boston, Washington, Cleveland, and Pittsburgh and the New York Times radio station also carried the debate live. The Canadian Broadcast Company ran the debate on tape delay. The debate was held in Charleston at WCHS with news director Bill Ames as the moderator. W. E. "Ned" Chilton, III, assistant to the editor of the *Charleston Gazette* and Dale Schussler of WTRF in Wheeling joined Ames to ask the candidates questions submitted to the paper by West Virginia voters.

In his opening remarks, Humphrey focused on Republican

policies and stated that Richard Nixon should not be the next president of the United States. Kennedy applauded the people of West Virginia and noted that the state needed help to develop economically. Humphrey found little to disagree with but, instead, took the opportunity to tout his foreign policy experience, especially his meeting with Soviet leader Khrushchev and to state his concern for the United States stance in its global competition with the Soviet Union. Kennedy stated his concern for those who were forced to used public assistance and surplus, even producing a can of powdered eggs to demonstrate his point.

For many, especially the press, the debate was a disappointment because the sparing, jabs and harsh rhetoric of campaign trail had been abandoned in front of the television cameras. Instead both candidates put forth their gentle side and saved their criticism for the Eisenhower Administration, Nixon and Republicans.

Humphrey and Kennedy mostly agreed on the issues, even at times sharing answering duties for questions posed by the panel that asked if congressional Democrats bore some responsibility for the conditions in West Virginia. The most disagreeable part of the debate came near the end when a question was asked of Humphrey if he thought he could win the nomination. Humphrey responded that the election was far from over and that any Democrat who believed they had a lock on the convention was wrong. Kennedy responded by saying. "No one knows who is going to win, but I would say that it may well be decided in West Virginia."

In closing, Kennedy pointed out to voters and the press that many people supporting Humphrey were not necessarily strong supporters, but were voting for Humphrey to stop Kennedy. He reiterated that voters could do with their votes as they wished, but he wanted to ensure that the point was made. For his closing words and in response Humphrey tried to differentiate himself from Kennedy. He said that he welcomed the support of West Virginia voters and that during the campaign he never complained about a gangup taking place. With that, the first televised presidential primary debate came to an end.

In the aftermath, Republicans complained to the television stations which aired the debate. They argued that according to the television fairness doctrine, a provision of the Federal Communications Commission that required equal time for televised political discussions and debates, Republicans should be given equal time. West Virginia national committeeman Walter S. Hallanan urged Republican National Chairman Senator Thruston Morton of Kentucky to write letters of protest to the stations and networks to allow a Republican rebuttal to the charges of Kennedy and Humphrey. From the Republican perspective, "There was no debate, no controversy, no difference of opinion. The so-called debate was a political fraud upon the network and the American people." A defiant Hawthorne Battle, president of WCHS, denied Morton's request for equal time and said that he was surprised by the senator's attack on free speech rights. Battle further explained that he would have provided equal time to Republicans if any of them were on the ballot in the West Virginia primary. NBC and Westinghouse also denied Morton's request, but the Mutual Broadcasting Company agreed to provide equal time.

Following the debate, Humphrey left Charleston and headed to the state's northern panhandle. The following day, May 5, Humphrey embarked on an eleven-hour tour. His day began in Weirton, followed by visits to Wellsburg, Bethany, downtown Wheeling, Wheeling College and finished in Morgantown with a speech at West Virginia University. In Weirton, Humphrey was presented with a steel key to the city by Mayor David T. Frew. Following the presentation Humphrey told the crowd that there needed to be federal standards for unemployment compensation and that his 10 Point Economic Plan included just such a provision. At Wellsburg Humphrey responded to a report that West Virginia Governor Cecil Underwood had announced that President Eisenhower urged federal agencies to address the problems in West Virginia. Humphrey answered the news with a blunt and boisterous question, "Mr. President, where have you been?" At Bethany, Humphrey was greeted by his most enthusiastic crowd of the day. Following his speech, the Bethany crowd called him back to the stage three times before he departed for Wheeling.

In Wheeling, Humphrey spoke to a crowd in front of the Wheeling Post Office Building where a reporter asked him about the charges waged by Republicans that his debate with Kennedy violated the fairness doctrine. Humphrey made light of the charges by saying that he would love to debate Vice President Nixon and that both he and Kennedy could defeat him. At Morgantown Humphrey spoke before students and faculty at West Virginia University. During his speech Humphrey suggested that electric power plants should be moved closer to the mines. With this approach the state could power the East coast and increase the prosperity of the state's residents.

Meanwhile, Kennedy made his third visit to Beckley where he criticized Governor Underwood and his recent calls for Kennedy and Humphrey to leave the state. Following his Beckley visit, Kennedy moved on to Collins High School for a second visit to the school. He delighted the students when he told them that he returned to the school because they had "the best cheering section of any high school in the United States." Later in the day, Kennedy spoke to a crowd of 3,000 people at the Charleston Civic Center and made a visit to West Virginia State College. The West Virginia State visit was marked by a rare campaign planning mistake by the Kennedy team, when Kennedy, still hampered by a sore throat, was forced to address the audience without the benefit of a public address system. He then rushed back to Charleston for a television appearance, but there was more confusion when Kennedy showed up at the wrong television station. At day's end, Kennedy and Humphrey both left the state to return to Washington to vote in the Senate on the Area Redevelopment Bill, a bill that both candidates were touting as a cure for West Virginia's economic woes.

While the West Virginia campaign was drawing attention

across the nation, an article showing the darker side of politics in the state appeared in a Life magazine. The article entitled, "A Small State Takes the Limelight" was written by *Life* correspondent Donald Wilson. Wilson quoted local lawyer Dan Dahill, who told him that in Logan County any man could be elected for $5,000, except for the office of county sheriff, which would require $40,000. Referring to Logan County as an example of the "Bible Belt" of West Virginia that made up one-third of the state's Democrats, Wilson explained that along with vote buying at from $2 to $5 per vote, half-pints of moonshine or liquor were used to secure votes. He further explained that local candidates also used "slating" or the printing of lists of candidates to influence voters on Election Day. If these failed, Wilson told his readers that "lever brothers," or local poll workers, could make the voting machines sing a favorable tune. The final part of the article addressed the question of religious bigotry in West Virginia. To make his point, Wilson interviewed Bob Dingess, the local political official at the Smokehouse Fork Precinct, who explained that he probably would not vote for Kennedy because he was Catholic. This view, Wilson said, was less prevalent in the younger generation, but still prominent of the older people in the community who had ties to the defunct Ku Klux Klan, like former Klan organizer and sitting Judge C.C. Chambers. While rumors about voting fraud and payoffs were swirling around the campaigns, tangible evidence or prosecutable proof, or a willingness to thoroughly investigate and prosecute vote-buying charges never surfaced.

Both candidates returned to the campaign trail in West Virginia on Friday, May 6. Kennedy flew to Huntington and met with voters in Ceredo and Kenova before flying back to Charleston for a television appearance. The Kennedy camp also had to do some damage control over reports that FDR, Jr., had questioned Humphrey's lack of military service during World War II. Reporters quickly questioned both campaigns. The first questions were to FDR, Jr., who was asked by reporters if he was calling Humphrey a "draft dodger." Roosevelt responded that was not what he said and that he "deeply resented" the characterization of his words. He also encouraged reporters to check the record. Kennedy quickly distanced himself from the charges and explained that he did not approve them and that he believed that it should not have been a part of the campaign. Humphrey, the experienced politician that he was, would not respond to the baiting of reporters eager for a juicy story. With that, the story quickly died as neither candidate wanted to deal with the controversy with Election Day only a few days away.

Humphrey's first stop after returning to West Virginia on May 6 was in Welch where he addressed economic issues. He was forced to abandon other scheduled stops in McDowell County because of an important dinner in Wyoming County at Pineville High School in honor of Judge R. D. Bailey, the first supporter in West Virginia to stump for Franklin Roosevelt in 1932. At the dinner, Humphrey railed on the extravagance of the Kennedy campaign in West Virginia. He followed those charges with glowing remarks about FDR. Following Humphrey, Robert Kennedy took to the podium and told the people in the audience that if the United States had the money to rebuild West Germany then it also had the money to rebuild West Virginia. The most intriguing question of the night was addressed to California Congressman James Roosevelt, the son of FDR, who was asked about his brother's support of Kennedy in the West Virginia primary. An astute politician in his own right, the congressman explained that in the Roosevelt family, everyone was able to support whoever they wished.

As the rain fell on May 7, Kennedy made stops in Charleston and Elkview before giving a speech at the Jackson County Courthouse in Spencer. In a funny twist, the rain was so persistent that Kennedy purchased a hat for $2.02 from a local clerk ironically named Truman to cover his trademark hair. A Boston Globe reporter purchased the hat from Kennedy. Following his speech in Spencer, Kennedy returned to Charleston for a flight to Nebraska for the presidential primary that was also scheduled for May 10.

While Kennedy was busy flying to Nebraska, one of his major rivals for the presidential nomination was heading for Clarksburg. While he did not appear on the ballot in West Virginia or other states, Senate Majority Leader Lyndon Johnson of Texas was the favorite of many in West Virginia. Johnson was the guest speaker at the state's largest annual Democratic fundraiser, the Jefferson-Jackson Dinner. The dinner had also been a stopping place for Kennedy, who had handled the same duties to great fanfare in 1958, and Stuart Symington another presidential contender who headlined the 1959 dinner.

When Johnson arrived in West Virginia he had the state's two senators in tow. Robert Byrd was Johnson's most outspoken and vocal supporter in the state. Jennings Randolph was more cautious than Byrd and less revealing of his true loyalties, but his role as toastmaster left little doubt of where he would stand if Johnson was the eventual nominee. FDR, Jr., attended the dinner on behalf of the Kennedy camp and told of his support for the Massachusetts senator. Humphrey, however, arrived to the dinner late, as he had been through most of his campaign, to greet the 500 people who had assembled.

Johnson's visit to Clarksburg illustrated the larger scope of the presidential nomination process. While the eyes of the nation were watching the primary in West Virginia, the maneuvering of the candidates for the nomination was brought to light. Johnson's visit interjected his presence in the state just prior to the election where many of his supporters hoped he would boost Humphrey in the state and derail Kennedy's bid. While organizers of the event told the press that planning for the event began in 1959, few could deny the enormous shadow that Johnson cast on the primary in West Virginia. The impact was never more prominent than in the pages of the *Clarksburg Exponent* whose coverage of the event dominated the paper in their Election Day issue.

On Sunday, May 8, Kennedy returned to the state. He was scheduled to fly to Elkins with his wife Jacqueline, but inclement weather prevented the flight. Instead, Kennedy spoke to the crowd via telephone while FDR, Jr., was dispatched from Clarksburg to speak to the crowd at the Tygart Hotel. In a televised interview that evening on WCHS in Charleston, Kennedy's tone was much calmer and kinder than the campaign rhetoric of previous days. He said that he hoped that he and Humphrey would remain friendly when the campaigns were over. He further stated that he regretted the recent statements of those campaigning for him and that he felt Americans were not interested in those types of attacks. He explained that he believed that the people wanted a president who would not engage in that type of discussion but, instead, could deal with "sensitive and difficult matters." In closing, Kennedy stated that he expected to win the primary, but if he didn't, he had more primaries ahead to reach the nomination.

The Humphrey campaign, already running on fumes, planned a television call-in show on Sunday, May 8, to counter Kennedy's widespread presence on television. Humphrey's television budget was a pittance compared to the reported $34,000 that the Kennedy camp poured into television. News of his dwindling funds concerned the station management at WSAZ Channel 3, and they required that he pay in cash up front. Humphrey was forced to write a $750 check from his personal account to cover the cost. Journalist Theodore White, who saw the encounter between Humphrey and his wife Muriel, said it was a tragic scene because it appeared that the money for the show may have been earmarked for other purposes like his daughter's wedding that was scheduled a week following the primary. If the funding problem wasn't bad enough for Humphrey, the television show was a disaster. Without a screener for callers, the show that started with basic questions degenerated quickly as a Republican caller who was unhappy with the recent press coverage of West Virginia vehemently told Humphrey to get out of the state. The callers who followed rambled or went in directions that did not help Humphrey's cause. In the end, the show did nothing to help Humphrey and may have done more harm than good.

In spite of his dismal television performance the night before,

Humphrey hit the campaign trail early the next day. He spent his final day of the campaign visiting Kanawha and Putnam Counties. Humphrey continued to provide quips and one-liners and displayed the vigor and positive energy that was his nature.

On the final full day of the West Virginia campaign, Kennedy began his day with stops in Cabell County and Huntington before flying to the Wood County Airport to spend the rest of the afternoon in Parkersburg. In late afternoon he returned to Charleston. During the day Kennedy promised via television that, if victorious, he would submit legislation within 60 days to help the people of West Virginia. Reporters on the campaign remarked that the usual Kennedy confidence was absent on this day and the senator seemed a little gloomy.

The newspapers of West Virginia issued a collective sigh of relief that Election Day had finally come. The *Charleston Gazette* displayed a cartoon on the front page that showed a West Virginia voter under the watchful eye of television cameras making his way to the polls with the thought that he would finally get his say. The primary had been intense. The spectacle had reached every corner of the state with the candidates, their families and friends, and supporters stopping by and pushing their man in the race. Reporters from newspapers, radio and television had put West Virginia on a national stage "warts and all." All that was left was to tally the votes and announce the winner.

On May 10, Election Day, Kennedy and Humphrey both left West Virginia in the early morning for Washington to speak to the same Democratic women's group. Following his speech Humphrey returned to Charleston. While Kennedy, his family, FDR, Jr., and his campaign workers told crowd after crowd of their utmost confidence on Election Day, doubts remained. The campaign in West Virginia had been brutal, and the Kennedy camp had poured untold resources and had spent unknown sums; however, the question remained, would it be enough? Unsure of success, Kennedy decided to remain in Washington to avoid the spectacle that he would be forced to endure following a defeat.

With Kennedy in Washington, his brother Bobby was left to watch the vote totals roll in at the Kanawha Hotel. Kennedy, meanwhile, joined his wife and a couple of friends for dinner and a movie. Humphrey waited at the Ruffner Hotel. The polls closed at 8:00 pm and the first results trickled in around 9:00 pm. By 10:00 pm, the rout was on statewide. Humphrey, realizing defeat, began to contact his supporters and contributors across the country to announce the grim news.

John and Jackie Kennedy returned from their movie at 11:30 pm to find a note from the maid to call Charleston. Kennedy was delighted to hear from Bobby that the victory was going to be a landslide. He popped the cork on a bottle of champagne, called his father in Massachusetts, and headed for the airport to fly to Charleston to claim victory.

Word of Humphrey's concession reached the Kennedy headquarters at 1:00 am. Bobby Kennedy made a personal call on Humphrey and escorted him in the rain to his campaign headquarters on Capitol Street for his concession speech. In a tearful scene Humphrey announced that he was no longer a candidate for the Democratic nomination. Following his brief words, Humphrey made his way with Bobby to the Kanawha Hotel to await the arrival of the victor.

By 3:00 am, Kennedy had made his way to Charleston. In his speech, he said that he was indebted to the people of West Virginia. He later expressed his gratitude that they had finally put an end to the religious question. In a prepared passage he reiterated his commitment to the people of West Virginia by saying, "I want to pledge again that I will not forget the people of West Virginia nor will I forget what I have seen and learned here. On my television broadcast last night, I said that if elected President I would immediately inaugurate a program of help for West Virginia. This I will do."

For Humphrey, his presidential hopes in 1960 ended in West Virginia. As reporters asked who he would support following his defeat, Humphrey refused to show his hand. Members of his campaign, still stinging from the nastiness of the past few weeks, told reporters that they would most likely support Adlai Stevenson for the nomination. The final insult to the Humphrey campaign in West Virginia was a parking ticket on the Humphrey tour bus, placed by a local policeman who had overlooked the illegally parked bus during the campaign, but now saw no reason to look the other way.

In the official results Kennedy defeated Humphrey by a margin of 236,510 to 152,187. The 60.8 percent to 39.2 percent victory represented a landslide for Kennedy. He won 50 of the state's 55 counties. Only Cabell, Doddridge, Hampshire, Lincoln and Putnam counties gave Humphrey modest victories. In spite of the lopsided total, Humphrey had a strong showing in most counties. Even with the strong showing in West Virginia, Kennedy's battle for the nomination was far from over. While Humphrey was removed as serious contender, Lyndon Johnson and Adlai Stevenson were names still being considered by many Democrats. Kennedy's victory in West Virginia did, however, undermine the candidacy of Senator Stuart Symington. In West Virginia Kennedy demonstrated his ability to woo voters that Symington was counting on for support.

The Conventions

John Kennedy had made strong showings in primaries across the country, but even as delegates made their way to Los Angeles for the Democratic National Convention in 1960, his nomination was still in doubt. Even West Virginia's delegates were undecided, in spite of Kennedy's stunning victory in May. The delegates from West Virginia were not bound to support the winner of the primary and many of them were, in fact, actively working for other candidates. The most notable of these delegates was Senator Robert Byrd who was still strongly entrenched in the Johnson camp, but when a *Charleston Gazette* reporter polled the delegation in Los Angeles there were many who were cool to the Johnson nomination because they did not believe he could beat Nixon. Others in the delegation were still loyal to Adlai Stevenson.

As the convention got underway Byrd remained staunch in his support of Lyndon Johnson. When interviewed, he said that the nomination was far from being Kennedy's. He further stated that he wouldn't join the Kennedy bandwagon and that it would have to run him over. When the reporter asked him about his support of Johnson, Byrd responded that there were only three things that would prevent him from doing so: "One would be for Sen. Johnson to withdraw as a candidate, which I'm sure he will not do. Another is that if Sen. Johnson should have a heart attack. The third is that if I should have a heart attack."

As the delegates filled the convention hall, all knew that the hopes of Stevenson, Johnson and Symington depended on Kennedy not receiving the nomination on the first ballot. As the voting began the Kennedy camp knew it took 761 delegates to receive the nomination. If he did not get it on the first vote, many state delegations would be free to abandon him and vote for another choice. As the state roll call began, Alabama gave Johnson 20 delegates and Kennedy 3. At Washington, Kennedy had reached 710 delegates. The West Virginia delegation voted 15 for Kennedy, 5 ½ for Johnson, 3 for Adlai Stevenson, and 1 ½ for Stuart Symington. Wisconsin made Kennedy's total 748. Wyoming finally ended the tension by casting all 15 of its votes for Kennedy. The final total had Kennedy with 806 votes; Johnson 409; Symington 86; Stevenson 79 1/2; and all others 140 ½.

With the nomination in hand, Kennedy had to decide on a running mate. In a surprise to many, Kennedy announced that Lyndon Johnson would be his Vice Presidential choice. Even more surprising for reporters in West Virginia was Kennedy's swift moves to unite the party. The shocker for the cynics of the newsroom was the invitation sent from Kennedy to Senator Robert C. Byrd to join him on the stage as he formally received the nomination. Byrd had been the most vocal and outspoken of anyone in West Virginia in his attempts to derail the Kennedy nomination. Byrd, who had already left Los Angeles when word came of Kennedy's invitation, was 135 miles away, expressed regret for missing the occasion, but vowed to support Kennedy in his efforts to become the 35th president of the United States. With that, the Democratic Party of West Virginia mended the wounds that were opened by the primary and convention battles and joined together to defeat Nixon in the fall.

Within two weeks Republicans held their national convention in Chicago. With little surprise the party chose Vice President Richard Nixon to head the ticket. For West Virginia a great honor was given to Republican Governor and U. S. Senate candidate Cecil Underwood when he was chosen to be a keynote speaker during the convention. Underwood used his speech to criticize Democratic policies, especially Kennedy and Humphrey for their campaigns in West Virginia. However, Underwood was disturbed when Nixon urged him to cut the punch line of his speech that was aimed at Kennedy's choice of his former rival Johnson because Nixon, himself, was considering adding his formal rival New York Governor Nelson Rockefeller to the ticket to broaden his appeal. Nixon, however, bypassed Rockefeller and, instead, chose former Massachusetts Senator and United Nations ambassador Henry Cabot Lodge, Jr., to join the ticket.

With the nominees picked, both political parties geared up for a highly competitive general election. The campaign that followed was very different from those that came before it and it changed the face of American elections.

The General Election

Following the conventions, both candidates and their running mates crossed the country trying to secure voters. In West Virginia, the campaign duties were mostly left to surrogates except for two high profile visits by Kennedy and Nixon. On September 19, Kennedy returned to West Virginia to attend a day-long conference dedicated to employment. The conference was headlined by key officials from 10 states to address the economies of depressed areas and highlighted ways to create new jobs and new growth. Kennedy's address at the closing of the conference placed the blame of the country's economic woes directly on Republicans. He further mocked and criticized Nixon, who he said was touting the success of an American economy that left many people suffering. Kennedy ended his speech with the idea that for America to go forward and for freedom to flourish everyone need to benefit economically.

Not to be outdone, Nixon and the Republicans gathered in Charleston the day following the first televised Kennedy-Nixon debate. During his speech Nixon took the opportunity to address recent statements made by Kennedy. The vice president said that many of Kennedy's statements had been used by foreign communist newspapers to criticize the United States. In the latter half of the speech Nixon urged Kennedy to move above partisan politics and glib promises. Finally, he urged voters to support the Republican ticket and Cecil Underwood in his campaign for the Senate.

Kennedy received a huge boost to his campaign when former First Lady Eleanor Roosevelt made a campaign swing through West Virginia. Mrs. Roosevelt landed in Bluefield and made several stops on her way to Charleston where she met with reporters and gave several speeches in support of Kennedy. Mrs. Roosevelt had been a staunch supporter of Adlai Stevenson in the past few elections and even held pat in the current, but following the nomination of Kennedy she publicly supported Kennedy and had some criticism for Nixon.

On the same day that the former First Lady was in Charleston, Lyndon Johnson made a visit to Huntington. Hampered by bad weather and forced to move into the circuit court room of the Cabell County Courthouse, Johnson warned the assembled crowd of 1,100 that the Republicans had become desperate and that they would most likely be issuing a "sneak punch" in the days leading up to the election. He also told the crowd that Republicans were using New York Governor Nelson Rockefeller to appeal to northern voters, while the conservative Republican Senator Barry Goldwater in the Southwest and they both were telling voters very different stories. He ended his speech by reminding West Virginians that they had a friend in John Kennedy and that he always felt as though he was West Virginia's third senator.

The frantic nature of the campaign drew silent as voters across the country made their way to the polls. The election proved to be one of the closest elections in United States history. In the end Kennedy was able to secure enough votes in the Electoral College to defeat Nixon. Voters across the country were forced to go to bed on Election Night without a clear winner. In the early hours of the next morning the candidates were notified that Kennedy had won. Nixon, however, made the Kennedys wait throughout the morning for his concession speech. When time came for the concession it was not Nixon who announced his concession, but instead his press secretary Herb Klein.

The Presidency

West Virginia again gave Kennedy a boost when state voters gave him 52.7 percent of the vote. In the few years that he was in office, Kennedy was true to his promise made on the eve of the West Virginia primary when he said that he would not forget the debt he owed the state. During his administration's thousand days, and beyond, millions of dollars were funneled into West Virginia for roads, federal projects, and other programs that made a huge impact.

Kennedy always spoke of the honor and dedication to country that was the goal of his life's work. When he spoke of West Virginia, he always noted the abundance of those traits in the people that called the state home. He reveled in the state motto that "mountaineers are always free," and that the people of the state were more than willing to do more than their fair share to protect the freedom of the entire nation. Kennedy words echoed what West Virginians had always known about themselves, but few from beyond the state's jagged borders understood. The pinnacle of the relationship between Kennedy and the state occurred during the state's centennial celebration in June 1963, when from the steps of the state capitol in front of a crowded lawn, the president, noting the rainy weather, said words that still ring in the ears of those present that day. He said, "The sun doesn't always shine in West Virginia, but the people do."

Tragically, a few months following the West Virginia Centennial Celebration, news echoed across the country first that Kennedy had been shot, and later that he had died. For many in West Virginia who turned out to meet Kennedy and who saw him speak from the Capitol steps only months before, it was like they had lost not only a good friend to West Virginia, but a member of their immediate family. The loss was immense and devastating. In the years that have passed the Kennedy legacy has remained and his memory continues to lives on.

Sources

Online Resources:
 For the most complete set of resources on the 1960 West Virginia Presidential Primary visit the online exhibit produced by the West Virginia Archives and History Section on the West Virginia Division of Culture and History entitled: Battleground West Virginia: Electing the President in 1960. To access the website go to:
http://www.wvculture.org/history/1960presidentialcampaign/1960presidentialcampaign.html

Published Sources:
Gary A. Donaldson, *The First Modern Campaign: Kennedy, Nixon, and the Election of 1960*. Lanham, Maryland: Rowan & Littlefield Publishers, 2007.

Kenneth S. Davis, *A Prophet in His Own Country: The Triumphs and Defeats of Adlai E. Stevenson.* New York: Doubleday and Company, 1957.

Kenneth S. Davis, *The Politics of Honor: A Biography of Adlai E. Stevenson.* New York: G. P. Putnam's and Son, 1967.

Daniel B. Fleming, *Kennedy vs. Humphrey, West Virginia, 1960: The Pivotal Battle for the Democratic Presidential Nomination.* Jefferson, N.C.: McFarland, 1992.

Herbert J. Muller, *Adlai Stevenson: A Study in Values.* New York: Harper and Row Publishers, 1967.

David Pietrusza, *1960 - LBJ vs. JFK vs. Nixon: The Epic Campaign that Forged Three Presidencies.* New York: Union Square Press, 2008.

Theodore H. White, *The Making of the President 1960.* New York: Atheneum Publishers, 1961.

7

Innovation and the Kanawha Valley Salt Industry[7]

While West Virginia is most noted for its coal resources, the state was once home to a thriving salt industry that developed near Malden on the Kanawha River near Charleston. Long forgotten by many, the industry was not only a national leader in salt production, but also a place where mountain state innovators made huge technical contributions to the salt industry and revolutionized other extractive industries in the process.

For centuries buffalo and other wild game gathered near the current site of Malden on the Kanawha River. Known as the Great Buffalo Lick, the area became a source of salt for prehistoric people, European hunters, and, following the American Revolution, permanent settlers. The first commercial use of the salt marshes began in 1797 when Elisha Brooks opened a small furnace on land leased from Joseph Ruffner. The crude operation reduced brine to salt and produced around 150 pounds a day. In 1802, two sons of Ruffner inherited the property. They sank a sixty foot well

---

[7] A version of this article appeared in the Summer 2010 issue of West Virginia Executive Magazine.

using hollow sycamore trees as casings to access higher concentrations of brine, and with that, they increased their output to 1,250 pounds of salt per day. Today, metal casings have replaced the sycamore trees used by the Ruffner brothers, but their use remains an important part of subterranean drilling today.

The real boost for salt production in the Kanawha Valley began as a result of the War of 1812. An embargo was placed on British salt and producers along the Kanawha were more than willing to fill the void. By 1815, fifty-two salt producers lined the banks of the river, pushing annual production to 640,000 bushels, and making the area the premiere salt producing area in the country. With this rapid expansion, salt makers turned to the cheapest source of labor at the time—slaves. The number of slaves in Kanawha increased from 352 in 1810 to a top figure of 3,140 in 1850. The use of industrial slavery was unique to the salt industry because most slaves in the United States were never used in industrial operations. Also in contrast to agriculture, most slaves used in the salt industry were not owned by the company, but instead, leased from their owners for work at the furnaces and in the mines.

When the War of 1812 ended, British producers flooded the United States with their salt. The salt supply greatly exceeded demand and the price of salt fell dramatically. Through lease and purchase the Donnelly and Steele Company moved to consolidate salt properties on the Kanawha River and control the market, but they were unable to control more than twenty-five percent. Nevertheless, in 1817 the major producers in the valley formed the Kanawha Salt Company, a legal group created to control the output of salt from Kanawha Valley salt makers. As historian John Stealey notes in his book, *The Antebellum Kanawha Salt Business and Western Markets*, the new collective was not technically a trust as many local historians have reported and repeated, but instead a very early example of an output pool or a collective. While producers were willing supporters of the collective in 1817, over time the collaborative effort fell apart. Later attempts to control output also failed when disagreements erupted over production amounts and when some local producers failed to join the pool.

Yet, prior to 1825, salt producers of the Kanawha Valley had a great advantage over the competing regions because of the easy access they had to the Ohio and Mississippi Rivers, especially the meat packing center of Cincinnati. The transportation advantage, however, would last only for a few years. Canal building in New York and Ohio gave many areas greater access to western markets. But in spite of the increased competition, Kanawha producers remained competitive thanks to innovation.

With wood as the major construction material, maintenance and repair were an incessant part of the salt business. New methods and materials were readily tried, and if successful, adopted. Within the close confines of the Kanawha Valley innovations spread quickly. For example, salt maker David Ruffner first used coal as a fuel source in salt production in 1817. Within a few years every producer in the Kanawha Valley had converted its furnaces to the new fuel that provided a more intense heat. The conversion coincidentally ignited coal mining in the region and gave producers along the Kanawha an economic advantage that other regions could not match for decades.

While coal gave producers an advantage, an innovation by William "Uncle Billy" Morris in 1831 propelled salt production in the Valley to its greatest heights and revolutionized subterranean drilling by solving a problem that had hampered drilling up until its invention. One of the most difficult challenges for drillers in these early days was that the drill tip would become lodged or stuck far below ground. It proved to be very difficult to dislodge them, especially the deeper they went. To prevent this from happening, Uncle Billy devised a slipping connector made of iron, called "slips" or "jars," that attached to the drilling bit. The addition of the slips created a sideways motion that would dislodge the bit when it was lifted upward. The invention was a simple solution, and it revolutionized drilling, allowing deeper wells. Producers then had new access to higher concentrations of salt which reduced processing times. Uncle Billy never patented his solution, but following his work in the Kanawha Valley salt industry, he moved on to Western Pennsylvania where his innovation helped to launch the fledgling oil industry.

The pinnacle of salt production in the Kanawha Valley was in 1846 with 3,224,786 bushels of salt. In spite of this immense production, the following decades weren't so kind to the industry. First, the Panic of 1857 had a severe and adverse impact on salt producers along the Kanawha. Flooding in September 1861 fouled salt wells and destroyed furnace buildings, many of which were never rebuilt. For those companies that could rebuild, expansion of the U. S. railroad network following Civil War transformed the salt market. The city of Chicago rose as the country's hog butcher, replacing Cincinnati, the major outlet and consumer for Kanawha salt. By the 1870s salt produced elsewhere reduced demand further. Investors also abandoned the industry and instead invested heavily in coal mining ventures. By 1907 only the Dickinson Company at Malden remained and production dropped to one-third of the industry's peak. Just when it looked like the industry was headed for a steady decline into the annals of history, events on the world stage once again transformed the Kanawha Valley salt industry.

Prior to 1914, America relied heavily on the German chemical industry, but as World War I erupted in Europe, the United States, as it had done during the War of 1812, turned to the Kanawha Valley for the salt needed to produce chemicals for the war effort. The U.S. government built the first two major chemical plants in the Kanawha Valley, with a high explosives plant at Nitro and a mustard gas plant at Belle. Shortly after the war, Union Carbide, DuPont, and other chemical firms took up residence in the Kanawha Valley. The Kanawha Valley was no longer a center for salt production, but, instead, became a leader in chemical production.

While the salt industry in West Virginia lasted for a little more than 100 years, the industry provided numerous innovations. The Ruffner brother's sycamore gum casings and Uncle Billy's jars are viewed by historians of the drilling industry as monumental achievements. The Kanawha Salt Company in recent years has come to the attention of historians who had previously dated the rise of output pools, trusts and monopolies after the Civil War. Furthermore, the industry demonstrates that the pages of West Virginia history are home to many innovators just waiting to be brought to light.

Bibliography

Mark Kurlansky. *Salt: A History of the World.* New York: Walker and Company, 2002.

Rice, Otis and Stephen Brown. *West Virginia. A History.* Lexington: University of Kentucky Press, Second Edition 1993.
Stealey, John E. III. *The Antebellum Kanawha Salt Business and Western Markets.* Lexington: The University of Kentucky Press, 1993.
Stealey, John E. III. *The Kanawhan Prelude to Nineteenth-Century Monopoly in the United States.* Richmond, Va.: Virginia Historical Society, 2000.

8

Hanger's Limb[8]

J. E. Hanger's mother was not thrilled when her 18-year-old son came home from Washington College in Lexington, Virginia, now known as Washington and Lee, and reported that he intended to enlist in the Confederate Army in the spring of 1861. After all, she had other sons who had already gone to join the Southern forces. She sent him off reluctantly, instructing him to go to the Churchville Cavalry unit under the command of Colonel George Porterfield in western Virginia where he would at least have the companionship of two of his brothers.

This seemingly unremarkable moment was the beginning of events both historic and consequential. Hanger would become the first man wounded by a cannon ball in the American Civil War and the first to have a limb amputated. A practical and resourceful man, he invented an effective prosthetic leg with a movable joint and then started what would become the largest artificial limb company in the world.

Following the attack on Fort Sumter in April 1861, General George McClelland planned to move to support the pro-Union populace of northwestern Virginia and secure the Baltimore and Ohio Railroad (B&O), which was of vital strategic importance to

---

[8] *A version of this article appeared in the* Winter 2011 *edition of* West Virginia Executive *Magazine.*

Northern forces. When word reached General McClelland that bridges on the B&O mainline were being burned by Confederate forces, he sent Colonel Benjamin Kelly of the Union's First Virginia Infantry to intercept. Colonel Kelly and his men found the Confederates gathered at Philippi in Barbour County. Hanger had not even officially enlisted in the unit when the Battle of Philippi, known as the first land battle of the Civil War, broke out.

Colonel Porterfield's unit was fairly quickly dislodged from Philippi by Union forces led by Colonel Kelly. The battle is sometimes referred to as the "Philippi Races" because of the enthusiasm with which the Confederate forces fled the area. Confederate forces were ill-equipped, and Hanger later recalled their stash of weapons as "loose ball powder and shot. Arms were flintlock muskets, horse pistols, a few shotguns and Colt revolvers."

Cannons were fired by Federal forces in the pre-dawn hours of June 3, 1861. Horses were stabled in the barn of Garret Johnson, where Hanger, only recently arrived, was acting as a sentry during the night. A six-pound cannon ball was fired at the barn and ricocheted off the doorframe, striking Hanger and badly mangling his leg. He crawled to the barn loft to hide and was discovered by Union troops and taken to the United Methodist Episcopal Church, which had been converted into a hospital by Union forces. There, Dr. James Robinson of the 16th Ohio Volunteers amputated Hanger's leg about seven inches below the hip bone, performing the first amputation of the Civil War. The amputation is described as having taken more than an hour without anesthesia. Hanger later said, "I cannot look back upon those days in the hospital without a shudder . . . No one can know what such a loss means unless he has suffered a similar catastrophe."

During the Civil War as many as 50,000 amputations were performed. At the start doctors were not well-prepared for what they would face. Most doctors who joined had never witnessed an amputation, let alone perform one. Of the 14,000 doctors who enlisted on either side, only slightly more than 500 had ever performed surgeries. While some accused doctors of unnecessary amputations, those amputations saved lives. When doctors hesitated, the patient often died of infection. Hanger's surgeon, however, had gained experience as a regimental surgeon during the Mexican War.

After his amputation Hanger was cared for locally by the William McClaskey family for two weeks and then relocated to the Thomas Hite farm. He was a prisoner of Federal forces for only a short while in Fort Chase, Ohio, and was exchanged at Norfolk in August 1861. Upon returning home, he began designing a useful limb. Artificial limbs had existed prior to the Civil War, but they consisted of a wooden post, not unlike a table leg, that was attached with a leather strap to the thigh or the clothing. This crude version of the human leg would not do for Hanger. He secluded himself in the second floor of his home where his family assumed he was despondent over his injury. Much to their surprise, Hanger descended the stairs upon a movable prosthetic leg in November 1861. He had invented the first artificial leg with a double-jointed articulating knee that used barrel staves and featured hinges at the knee and the foot.

After making limbs for other amputees, he went to Richmond where he was commissioned to make limbs for Confederate soldiers and where the Commonwealth of Virginia granted him a patent on his Hanger Limb. Later that year, he started J. E. Hanger Company in Richmond. Demand for his product brought the company great success, and in 1871 he relocated the company to Staunton, Virginia. That same year the U.S. Government granted Hanger a U.S. patent on his limb.

In 1873, Hanger married Nora Slater McCarthy of Richmond, Virginia. They had six sons and two daughters. A skilled mechanic with an inventive nature, Hanger patented many improvements to his limbs and the particular lathe used to manufacture them. He also invented a shampoo bowl and chair, an outdoor sleeping bed, an adjustable reclining chair, a water turbine, a Venetian window blind and even a horseless carriage which was played with as a toy by his children.

By 1888, Hanger's company headquarters was in Washington, D.C. World War I (WWI) increased demand for limbs in Europe and the company further expanded. Hanger spent 1915 in Europe studying the surgical experiences among the wounded of WWI. His company received special contracts with the French and the British governments. At his death in 1919 the company had offices in Philadelphia, St. Louis, Pittsburgh, Atlanta, London and Paris. During the company's long history, it created hundreds of prosthetic devices, manufacturing processes and orthotics. In 2011, the Hanger Company, now the Hanger Orthopedic Group, celebrated its 150th Anniversary, a milestone achieved by only an elite group of businesses. The company now has 4,300 employees and is valued at more than $800 million. J. E. Hanger's rise from adversity was nothing less than spectacular.

9

Clendenin, West Virginia, and the Birth of the Petrochemical Industry[9]

With the economic promise of Marcellus shale gas in West Virginia, industry leaders, state business development officials and eager investors have turned their focus towards development of downstream industries that use natural gas not only as a source of fuel, but also for the development of new products in the chemical industry.

While using natural gas as fuel is relatively straightforward, using it in the chemical industry requires a process in which hydrocarbon chains that make up the gas are broken or "cracked" to produce ethylene, propylene, butane and acetylene, which are collective known as olefins. Lately, there has been a great deal of talk about the building of a large scale "cracker" plant in West Virginia in the hope of further developing the petrochemical industry in the state. Few people know, however, that the petrochemical industry was created, developed and launched at a small plant along the Elk River right here in Clendenin, West Virginia. The large scale process of "cracking" was not only

[9] *A version of this article appeared in the Spring 2102 issue of* West Virginia Executive *Magazine.*

developed at the site, the plant's success gave rise to one of the largest chemical companies in the world -- Union Carbide.

Today, petrochemicals, chemicals produced from petroleum or natural gas, are commonplace, but prior to 1920 this was not the case. Chemicals produced before 1920 were produced using acetylene. Then some chemists, however, realized that ethylene would be better suited to produce a larger range of chemicals. Although the chemistry of ethylene was known prior to World War I, the chief source of it was derived by the dehydration of ethanol, which was expensive and did not produce large quantities. Efforts were made during the war to develop the process, but following the armistice many of those investigations were tabled. The efforts of a twenty-nine-year-old chemist, Dr. George O. Curme, Jr., at the Mellon Institute would revolutionize the production of ethylene through the cracking process and launch the petrochemical industry.

Early in the 20th century companies did not have independent research wings to develop new products and processes. In 1913, brothers Andrew and Robert Mellon launched the Mellon Institute of Industrial Research in Pittsburgh to address that need through company-sponsored fellowships. In 1917, three of these sponsored fellowships were combined. The senior fellow of the project was Dr. George O. Curme, Jr. The newly conceived fellowship charged researchers with the task of finding uses for ethylene, which was created during the production of acetylene by hydrocarbon cracking.

By the end of 1918, Union Carbide officials decided that there was need of a thorough review of the fellowship. In response, Dr. Curme and his associates provided company officials with projections. Edgar F. Price, a   vice-president of the company, pushed for the continuation of the research with a shift in emphasis from acetylene to ethylene derivatives for commercial and defense purposes. Work continued at the Mellon Institute in Pittsburgh and in Buffalo, New York, at Linde Air Products, which became part of Union Carbide in the 1917 consolidation. In

January 1920, the first ethylene was produced from the plant and further experimentation showed that it could be compressed without exploding. While progress was being made, a fire destroyed the Buffalo plant. Company officials decided that the research should continue at a new factory site.

Clendenin, West Virginia, was chosen, a town twenty miles above Charleston, West Virginia, on the Elk River. Officials were drawn to the area because of the Clendenin Gasoline Company, which was producing gasoline from natural gas through an absorption process. To profit from the byproducts of the process, they sold stripped-off methane to the United Fuel Gas Company, a local utility. The other volatile gases in the gasoline, namely ethane, propane and butane were allowed to "weather" off into the atmosphere in open vats. The volatile gasses that were escaping into the air were the same gases that were needed to manufacture ethylene and propylene through the cracking process. Carbide and Carbon Chemicals Corporation was formed and the new subsidiary purchased the plant and land nearby.

When construction began at Clendenin in 1920, many of the workers brought in from Pittsburgh and New York were put up in extra rooms in private homes nearby. The railroad ran by the plant and through Clendenin. Two passenger trains a day made the trip between Charleston and Clendenin. Each trip was torturous as the train wound its way along the Elk River making stops at every station along the line. Using the roads to get to Charleston was equally as challenging as many of them were only passable in the driest times of the year. Supplies and equipment had to be brought in by train, but the isolation helped the young men, mostly in their 30s, to focus on the work at hand. By 1921 construction was completed, and the real work began as the men who gathered at Clendenin tried to make their lab work a viable commercial enterprise.

The Clendenin plant was not established to be a full-scale manufacturing facility, but was instead to be a pilot plant intended to develop manufacturing processes for ethylene and ethylene derivatives. The major achievement at the plant was the development of a gas-fired refractory furnace that could be used to crack hydrocarbons in natural gas.

The process had been successful in the lab, but to be profitable the process had to be accomplished on a larger scale. The first ethane cracking furnace was fired at Clendenin in February 1921. The furnace burned natural gas that fired a circular configuration of copper-lined iron tubes. Butane and propane were cracked at a flow rate of 1,200 cubic feet per hour. After several configurations of the furnace which included a switch from the copper-lined tubes to longer chromium-iron pipes coupled with additional changes in the reactor configuration, ethylene production at the plant increased to cracked-gas rate of 15,000 cubic feet per hour. The advances proved that the furnace could provide the quantity of ethylene necessary to make the petrochemical industry successful.

In an effort to separate the ethane-propane-butane that was part of the natural gasoline process, stabilizer columns were developed. The columns were revolutionary in natural gasoline processing, moving the company to try to patent the process. When word of the columns spread, gasoline companies across the country quickly adopted the technology and the patents were eventually denied. Fortunately for the company, one of the gases that was separated was propane. Propane from the plant was initially planned as feedstock for the furnace. Efforts to develop a market for many of the new chemicals proved to be more difficult than expected, so bottled propane gas, marketed as Pyrofax, was sold to consumers as a source of gas for those who weren't connected to gas utilities. Sales of Pyrofax were successful and provided the bulk of the income for the subsidiary during its earliest years.

The main goal of the plant was still to develop ethylene products. The first large scale synthetic chemical product manufactured at Clendenin was the solvent Cellosolve. Cellosolve was used in the lacquer industry, mostly for automobile paints. With the success of Cellosolve, the plant at Clendenin finally proved that there was a market for products developed there and that they could be produced at a large scale.

Soon other products from the plant made their way to the marketplace. Ethylene glycol was produced that was initially used as a low temperature solvent for dynamite. Later, it was used as an anti-freeze for automobiles and marketed under the widely recognized trade name of Prestone. Other chemicals produced at the plant that included ethylene were used as a ripening agent for fresh fruits. Ethylene dichloride produced at the plant was used as a major dry cleaning fluid. Later dichloroethyl, marketed as Chlorex, was a solvent used for refining lubricating oils.

As the market for chemicals produced in Clendenin expanded, leaders of the company began to look toward the future. In 1923, a business study was commissioned to examine the costs of building new facilities in the Charleston area. The company began to look for property, and the idle Rollins Chemical Company in South Charleston was leased. Early in 1924 construction crews began work at the site. By 1925, cracking was halted at Clendenin and was moved to South Charleston where three dual-core furnaces were put into operation.

In the decade that followed more of the processes and chemicals that were developed at the Clendenin plant were moved to South Charleston and carried out at a dramatically larger scale. Many of the chemists that worked at Clendenin, the fathers of the petrochemical industry, moved to South Charleston and carried out their research, developing an astounding number of new chemical products. George Curme, Jr., whose research gave birth to the industry, became the vice-president of research and later a director on the board of the Union Carbide Corporation.

West Virginia leaders today are working diligently to build or attract a monumentally larger cracker plant. This plant might replicate the success of that group of chemists that began work in a small plant along the Elk River at Clendenin in the 1920s.

10

Paul Wissmach Glass Company[10]
A Survivor from West Virginia's First Natural Gas Boom

West Virginia has a colorful history especially when it comes to the glass industry. Few companies can boast of a more vibrant or prolonged history as the Paul Wissmach Glass Company in Paden City. Founded in 1903, the company today can produce more than 13,000 square feet of specialty glass a day in over 3,000 brilliant colors. Glass produced at their factory can be found at the White House, the Old Executive Office Building in Washington D.C., St. Peter's Basilica in Rome and in glass window installations and lamps around the world. While the family-owned company's catalog is impressive, equally remarkable is the fact that they are one of a very select few that have survived from West Virginia's first natural gas boom around the turn of the twentieth century.

The earliest record of West Virginia glass manufacturing can be traced to Wellsburg in 1810. By 1830, Wheeling boasted three glass companies, but glass manufacturing would spread no further until the 1890s when glass companies abandoned coal as the major fuel source and adopted natural gas. As companies converted, West Virginia became more attractive to the industry thank to cheap land and an abundance of natural gas. Companies from Ohio, Indiana

---

[10] *A version of this article appeared in the Fall 2011 issue of* West Virginia Executive *Magazine.*

and Pennsylvania moved to the state while new groups of investors built factories in northern West Virginia and along the Kanawha River Valley.

The resulting growth in manufacturing was remarkable. In 1890, West Virginia had seven glass factories with nearly 1,400 workers. Within a decade that number had surged to 16 companies with nearly 2,000 workers, and by 1905 the industry had expanded to 39 companies that represented 10 percent of the glass producers in the United States. In the 1920s the expansion continued, and West Virginia surpassed Indiana and Ohio to become the second largest glass producing state in the union.

The Paul Wissmach Glass Company's history begins with the company's namesake, a German immigrant living in New York City, who was importing stained glass from Europe. After seeing an ad for land along the Ohio River, Wissmach joined with another German immigrant Joseph Reininger in 1903 to create the Empire Glass Company in Paden City. Wissmach provided the capital and Reininger provided the know-how. The partnership between the men did not last very long, however, because in October 1904 Wissmach purchased Reininger's interest in the company and renamed it the Ohio Valley Glass Company.

The company continued to operate as the Ohio Valley Glass Company until a Board of Directors meeting on December 31, 1910. At that meeting the directors decided to change the name to Paul Wissmach Glass Company, to move the principal office of the company to New York City, and to double the number of shares of stock for the company.

Paul Wissmach led the company for another sixteen years until February 4, 1926, when he died at the age of 73 from what the doctors called a dilatation of the heart. By his side was his nephew Alfred Vollmar, who would assume the presidency of the company. A little over a year after Wissmach's death, the company faced another tragedy when a gas leak at the factory exploded and started a fire. The fire destroyed the section of the factory that produced cathedral art glass. At the time it was only the second such factory in the country and only one of three in the world. Efforts to fight the fire were both hampered and aided by a four-inch snow storm that both prevented outlying fire companies from responding and helped to dampen and suppress the blaze. Fortunately for the company, the wind kept the fire from spreading to the new section of the factory that produced rolled plate glass. Losses were estimated at $100,000, but insurance covered the damage and the company was able to reopen with new machinery and resume production a year later.

Once a fixture of manufacturing in West Virginia, the glass industry has fallen on hard times in the last fifty years. At Wissmach's, however, the glass business has remained much the same smaller family-run business as it began. Some of the major players in glass such as Fostoria and Libby-Owens-Ford, were purchased and closed in the 1980s, but Paul Wissmach Glass has survived. Mark Feldmeier attributes the long-term success of the company to a good quality glass at a remarkable price and "a conservative business strategy." The strategy has worked. Paul Wissmach is a world player in the art glass industry. Feldermeier explains that since 2008 much of his business has been exports to the Middle East and to Europe. His U.S. business has dropped since the economic downturn, as customers have limited the size of inventories, but Feldmeier expects improvement when the American economy rebounds.

Making glass is a hot business, both literally and figuratively. The factory has twelve brick furnaces that use natural gas to heat the limestone, soda ash and sand to 2,200 degrees. Different mixtures of ingredients create the distinct Wissmach colors. After heating, workers scoop the molten glass from the furnace and wheel it over to the glass press where a roller presses it into one of the 18 patterns that the company produces. The glass then travels down a 125-foot conveyor through a temperature controlled kiln called a lehr. The purpose of the lehr is to anneal the glass, or slowly and evenly cool it, to give glass it durability and to prevent shattering or heat-related breaking. At the end of the conveyor workers carefully remove the cooled sheet of glass and cut it to the appropriate size.

While the production process has changed little over the years, new processes and products are taking place at the factory. A process for fusing different colored glass pieces into a single piece, which would eliminate the need for metal banding between pieces of different colors, is becoming more widely available.

In mid-September of 2011, the company announced at the GlassBuild America expo in Atlanta, the addition of a line of temperable art glass that is available in eleven colors. Tempered glass is stronger and more durable. While tempered glass is commonly used in architectural glass doors, shower doors, refrigerator shelves and tables, the glass has not been available in a variety of colors. The company hopes to fill that gap in the market.

The Paul Wissmach Glass Company stands as one of the oldest glass companies still manufacturing in West Virginia, and one of the few companies that can trace its history to the state's first natural gas boom. Through good times and bad, the company has been able to weather devastating fires and economic storms. The company's long-term success and survival can be attributed to a willingness to stick to a plan that works and to carefully adapt to changes in the market. If they stick to that formula, it appears that the company will continue as President Mark Feldmeier says, "for the long haul."

11

West Virginia and the Miracle Drug[11]

When 53-year-old Henry McCulloch entered Fairmont General Hospital on January 14, 1944, any hope of his survival was slim. McCulloch had survived surgery to remove a tumor. His recovery was progressing normally and he was released from the hospital and returned home to Fairmont. In the days that followed, however, McCulloch began to have a high fever that resulted in his return to the hospital. Doctors at the hospital found that McCulloch's blood was infected with streptococcus and staphylococcus bacteria. Everyone at the hospital knew that death was to be the final outcome, unless they could administer the new and still experimental miracle drug, penicillin.

The modern history of penicillin began in September of 1928 when Scottish bacteriologist Alexander Fleming discovered that the mold had bacteria-killing powers. Widespread use of the mold as a drug proved elusive, however, because researchers were unable to develop a way to produce penicillin on a large scale. In 1941 with war raging across Europe, British scientists Howard Florey and Norman Heatley had fled the bombing of England and arrived in

---

[11] *A version of this article appeared in the* Winter 2011 *issue of* West Virginia Executive *Magazine.*

the United States with a stable and dried form of penicillin. In an effort to expand production the scientists were directed to a U.S. Department of Agricultural laboratory in Peoria, Illinois, to begin experiments. By March 1942, in spite of the efforts of researchers at the USDA and the major U.S. pharmaceutical companies, only a single dose of the drug produced by Merck and Company was available to treat a patient with a streptococcus infection. A month later 10 doses were available. Researchers struggled, but a breakthrough came after the discovery of penicillin on a cantaloupe in a Peoria, Illinois, market. The discovery propelled scientists to seek new mediums to grow the mold.

In the Mountain State researchers at West Virginia Wesleyan in Buckhannon joined the search and began experimenting with penicillin in January of 1944. Pure cultures of the mold were brought from a Pittsburgh hospital. Wesleyan chemistry professor Dr. Nicholas Hyam and Edward O'Hara of Weston tackled the medium problem by experimenting with potato water and corn steep liquor. By March, they had produced a crude form of penicillin using a large incubator built on the Wesleyan campus. In March 6, 1944, an article in the Fairmont Times reported that, at that time, Wesleyan was the only college in the U.S. experimenting with penicillin.

In Fairmont, doctors desperate to save McCulloch's life appealed to a leading penicillin researcher to help. Dr. C. S. Keefer of Evans Memorial Hospital in Boston had been working with penicillin for years and was known to provide the drug to civilians in extreme and life-threating circumstances. Fortunately for McCulloch, their appeal worked. Dr. Keefer agreed to send 10 vials of 100,000 units of the drug. Within 24 hours of the first shot of penicillin, McCulloch's fever had dissipated. After using eight vials of the drug and a six day stay in the hospital, the bacteria in his blood stream had been defeated. McCulloch was released. Doctors and nurses who had watched the episode closely were amazed by the "miracle recovery," but they would have to wait for several years before the drug was available for widespread civilian use.

The spring of 1944 marked a watershed point in the production of penicillin. Twenty-one fermentation plants, at the cost of one-million dollars each, were built in the U.S. and Canada. The plants were capable of producing 250,000 doses a month, much of that production reserved for military use. The first advertisement for penicillin was printed in the West Virginia Medical Journal in April 1944, a few months following Henry McCulloch's miracle recovery. The Commercial Solvents Corporation Pharmaceutical division placed a two-page ad in the journal describing their new facilities and explaining that in the future they would make the drug for civilian use

For the military, the first widespread use of penicillin was administered during the D-Day invasion on June 6, 1944. During the invasion nurses sprinkled a powdered form of penicillin on the wounds of soldiers. The drug made a major difference in the survival rate of soldiers and greatly reduced the number of amputations caused by infected wounds. Military officials reported that the drug increased the survival rate by 15%.

Following the war, penicillin continued to make a marked impact on public health. Another chronic health concern was the prevalence of venereal diseases. Prior to the widespread use of penicillin doctors were limited to treatments that were only somewhat effectual. In 1938, West Virginia's state health department reported that there were nearly 12,000 reported cases of syphilis. The author of the report noted that a true count was unrealistic, but those who received treatment received 80,334 doses of arsenicals, 86,144 doses of bismuth and 6,248 doses of mercury. Reported cases had increased dramatically as the state created free venereal disease clinics in counties across the state.

Of course, the problem of venereal diseases was not limited to West Virginia. Federal health officials were also looking for a way to combat these diseases. One of the more shocking proposals for a solution came in September of 1942, when Dr. N. R. Hon, assistant district director of the U.S. Public Health Service, made his way to West Virginia to discuss with state authorities a plan to convert abandoned Civilian Conservation Corp camps into internment camps for prostitutes, as a way to protect public health. Health Commissioner C. F. McClintic and Dr. S.L. Sisler of the state's venereal disease bureau had indicated that they would support the plan. While the plan may have received consideration by state and federal health officials, there is no evidence of the concept moving beyond the planning stages or weathering the political storm that would have assuredly erupted in the areas picked for the internment camps.

In April of 1948, Dr. Don Hatton of Huntington wrote an article on the treatment of syphilis with penicillin in the medical office. Prior to the article, penicillin injections required a 15 day stay in the hospital. Hatton reported in a very limited trial that injections in the office setting were promising. His words proved to be prophetic. With nearly 12,000 reported cases of syphilis in 1938, the number dropped to nearly 8,500 by 1947 as civilian use of penicillin became more prominent. Following Dr. Hatton's article in the journal in 1948, the number of cases had dropped to 5,211. By 1950 the number of reported cases had dropped to 2,692 cases.

In the years that have passed since penicillin made its debut, medicine has conquered many diseases, illnesses and maladies. Like the early experiments conducted at West Virginia Wesleyan, West Virginians have continued to play a role in medical research. With research conducted at our colleges, universities and research centers and the production of medicines and additives at our pharmaceutical companies and major chemical producers, the state has been a major contributor to furthering of medical research and to the improvement of the health of our nation and the world. When the doctors and nurses watched Henry McCulloch leave the hospital in 1944, they were amazed by his miraculous recovery and must have had hope for the future of medicine. Little could they imagine what the future would bring to the field and the role West Virginians would play in it.

12

A New Deal for West Virginia[12]

As a manufacturing state, West Virginia is often at the mercy of the ebb and flow of larger economic forces. The most dramatic of those swings took place in the late 1920s. While the economy was "roaring" in other parts of the country, in West Virginia things began to slow down years before the big crash on Wall Street. The Great Depression was particularly brutal and affected every aspect of the economy. For many counties in the state, the unemployment rate reached a staggering 80%.

People sought refuge from economic woes in political ideologies of many colors, but the presidential election of 1932 brought a dramatic shift in the American mindset for dealing with the effects of the Great Depression.

Franklin Roosevelt won handily, commanding 89% of the vote in the Electoral College. Democrats were elected in large numbers to the House of Representatives and the Senate as the country blamed President Hoover and the Republicans for the country's economic woes. Roosevelt instilled great hope in the citizenry with his inaugural speech on March 4, 1933 telling

---

[12] *A version of this article appeared in the Summer 2015 issue of* West Virginia Executive *Magazine.*

Americans, "the only thing we have to fear is fear itself." With majorities in Congress, Roosevelt began the New Deal.

In the 100 days that followed the inauguration, Congress reached its most productive period passing sweeping legislation that would change the shape of the United States government. The three prongs of the New Deal were to provide relief to the people suffering from the depression, recovery for industry and manufacturing, and reforms to address the systemic causes of the depression. Through a series of "alphabet soup" agencies, New Deal projects in West Virginia created new towns, established state parks, built bridges, dams, airports, post offices and stadiums, many of which are still in use today across the state.

The Civil Works Administration

One of the earliest programs of the New Deal was the Civil Works Administration. It was timed to provide relief for the unemployed as the winter of 1933 approached. The program put 80,000 West Virginians to work. Projects included road building, the construction of sanitary privies, and, in Morgantown, a manufacturing project that had women constructing mattresses. However, the costly Civil Works Administration was short-lived, brought to a close the following year.

Subsistence Homesteads

One of the more widely-known projects of the New Deal was the resettlement community of Arthurdale in Preston County. The impetus for the community began when reporter Lorena Hickok invited her friend First Lady Eleanor Roosevelt to Scotts Run, a collection of coal camps near Morgantown. Shocked by the conditions that she saw, the First Lady took an active role in the creation of a community that would ease the suffering of the people she met.

The back-to-the-land movement—the idea that workers would be more economically stable if manufacturing work were coupled with subsistence farming—formed the philosophy of the homestead concept. While the First Lady's involvement moved the project along, her presence also drew criticism. Cost overruns and early mistakes made national headlines including an exposé in the Saturday Evening Post. Some critics decried the cost, and still others argued that not enough people were helped. In total, 165 homes were built on the 1,200 acres purchased by the government. Along with the houses and farms, Arthurdale had a community center, post office, store, and school buildings. A factory that supporters hoped would provide steady jobs for the homesteaders was built, but attempts to find a permanent employer failed.

Arthurdale was not the only subsistence homestead in West Virginia. Tygart Valley Homestead, south of Elkins, included 202 homes, a community center, gas station and school. A limestone quarry and lumber mill were built to provide work for the homesteaders. In Putnam County the town of Eleanor, named for the First Lady, was built along the Kanawha River. The projects in Arthurdale, Tygart Valley and Eleanor may have failed to achieve to all that supporters of the program promised, but they did not fail the people who most desperately needed them. Buoyed by these communities, residents changed their economic station from one of perpetual poverty to one wherein progress was possible. Ultimately, the federal government began liquidating homestead communities in 1943, selling homes to private citizens through 1948. Today, most of the original houses in these communities are still standing.

Tygart Dam and Lake
One of the largest projects in West Virginia during the New Deal was Tygart Dam and Lake. Massive flooding and droughts had been common on the tributaries of the Monongahela River in the U.S. Army Corps of Engineers' Pittsburgh District, which included parts of Maryland, West Virginia, Pennsylvania and Ohio. The Public Works Administration began work on the project in 1935. Employing approximately 3,000 men in its construction, the 1,880-foot long dam required 324,000 cubic yards of concrete, more concrete than any other dam in the east. The dam was completed in 1938 and still controls over 1000 miles of watershed.

The Civilian Conservation Corps, State Parks and Forests
In 1933, Congress created the Civilian Conservation Corps to provide employment for young men in reforestation and recreation projects on local, state and federal lands. President Roosevelt was a staunch supporter of the program that included a philosophy of military-style discipline. In West Virginia more than 65 camps were established, with 55,000 men enrolled who each earned $30 a

month. In less than a decade the young men of the CCC built log cabins, trails, road ways, bridges, camp grounds, overlooks, fire towers, superintendent's residences, swimming pools, riding stables, and picnic shelters.

To carry out the program, the state created the Division of State Parks and purchased 30,000 acres of land. The first state park completed was Cacapon Resort State Park in Morgan County. The CCC built an 11-room lodge as well as dam, lake, and other recreational facilities. The largest of the log structures built in West Virginia is the Great Chestnut Lodge located at Camp Washington Carver. This lodge was originally built as an African American 4-H camp, the first of its kind in the nation. The breath-taking overlooks of Coopers Rock and Hawk Nests were projects carried out by the CCC. Today, visitors to the Monoghela National Forest, Capapon Resort, Lost River, Watoga, Babcock, Hawk's Nest, Holly River, Tomlison Run, Droop Mountain Battlefield can enjoy the labors of these men. The state forests of Cabwaylingo, Seneca, Kanawha, Kumbrabow and Coopers Rock also display their skills. The CCC ended in 1942 when many of the young men transitioned to military service in World War II. The benefit of their efforts, however, lives on in the beauty of West Virginia state parks and forests.

The construction projects of the New Deal changed the face of West Virginia; its programs reached every county in the state. Notable structures include city buildings in Sutton and Gassaway, Oakes Field in South Charleston, Benedum Airport in Harrison County, and the South Side Bridge that crosses the Kanawha River in Charleston. The old Parsons High School, Circleville School, and the elementary school building at the West Virginia School for the Deaf and Blind were constructed during the New Deal. Seventeen of the state's post office buildings were built during the period. Reminders of the New Deal can be found on plaques, set into stonewalls, and emblazed in the concrete of sidewalks. While some may debate the successes and failings of the New Deal, one only has to look around the state to see that many of the projects built during the period not only provided relief during difficult economic times but are still in use today.

ABOUT THE AUTHORS

Public historian Bryan Ward Jr. is a lifelong student of West Virginia history. He received degrees in history and education from West Virginia University in the 1990s. His work includes publications on Arthurdale and New Deal Communities, the 1960 West Virginia Presidential Primary, and numerous other West Virginia history-related topics. He is currently a history and government teacher in Southwestern Virginia.

Catherine Breese, a public school teacher for 20 years, holds a master's degree in English from James Madison University. She has taught American Literature and AP Language and Composition at the high school and college level. She is currently an information and technology resource teacher in Southwestern Virginia.

www.ingramcontent.com/pod-product-compliance
Lightning Source LLC
Chambersburg PA
CBHW031519040426
42445CB00009B/308